AWAY

By

Kevin Clarke

Copyright © 2018 Kevin Clarke

ISBN: 978-0-244-14152-3

Jo, my soul mate, without you none of it would have been possible, with you everything seems possible x

Megan, Jacob & Finlay, it's all been about you and for you and in return you have given us limitless joy, don't ever lose contact with each other.

Tracy, we are different, but it makes you no less special to me.

Rob, continual laughter and a continual friendship, always cherished.

Mum & Dad, you gave me an unbreakable foundation, I wish you were here for us to enjoy this together…

Acknowledgements

Nick for the first round of editing and grammar checking (it was CSE standard at best before that!).

Rob, Paul, Damien, Kieran, Sid, Rich, Dan J, Dan M, Dave, Ella, Katie, Nick, Ant & Gary for taking the time to read and feedback on the early drafts.

James for uttering the immortal words "I think there's a book in that Kev"

Tim for encouraging me and driving me on to turn 3 chapters into a book.

Nadia for the wonderful artwork and Martine for her generosity in taking the time out to create the cover.

& of course Jo, Megan, Jacob & Finlay for living and breathing it with me and helping me to tick off another item from the bucket list.

Finally, you as reader, thank you, you have got this far, so I'm hoping that you can see it through…

About Kevin Clarke

Kevin grew up in south-west London, before moving to Worthing in West Sussex with wife Jo and children Megan, Jacob and Finlay. This led to his introduction to Brighton and Hove Albion Football Club, then in League One; 12 years later the dream was realised - promotion to the Premier League.

Kevin's love of football also extended in his childhood to taping mock sporting interviews and commentaries with his school friend Bill. Those fond memories prompted him to enter talkSPORT's (a national sports radio station), five-month campaign in 2015 to find the UK's most talented fan to become the 'People's Pundit.'

Kevin's YouTube clip secured his spot into the next round and over the following four months there were a number of activities including being a weekly guest on the *Drive* show with Adrian Durham and Darren Gough, producing a short audio film, defending then Liverpool boss Brendan Rodgers live on air and self -sourcing interviews with Brighton manager Chris Hughton and former Uruguay, Chelsea and Spurs midfield player Gus Poyet.

Jeff Stelling from Sky Sports announced Kevin as the *People's Pundit* winner in May 2015 and his prize was to broadcast live for talkSPORT at Liverpool legend Steven Gerrard's last game for the club.

A number of spin off activities followed that including interviewing Peter Crouch, Ray Lewington (assistant coach for England working under Roy Hodgson) and former Liverpool and England goalkeeper David James on BT Sport. He also wrote a column for Brighton during their 2015-16 season.

Kevin then launched a series of *People's Pundit* podcasts with friend and local broadcaster Ian Hart. A YouTube version followed including interviews with George Dowell, chairman of Worthing FC in his 20s after a serious car accident had left him paralysed and wheelchair-bound and Mason Crane, England cricketer, before he headed off to the Ashes Tour.

Kevin's latest step in his 'hobby'; is this book (his first) about his experiences travelling to all 19 Premier League away games in Brighton's first season there along with his 17 year old son Jacob, where he also exposes one of football's biggest secrets – supporting 2 teams!

Foreword

Brighton & Hove Albion's promotion to the Premier League in 2018 meant different things to different people. For the directors, coaching staff and players, it was the reward for hard work over many years. For the fans who had watched the team in the bottom division during its exile in Gillingham, it was nothing less than a dream come true to watch the Seagulls take on clubs such as Arsenal, Manchester United and Tottenham Hotspur.

For me as a fan and a Brighton-based journalist working in the national press, it was a win-win. I could watch AND report on my own club in the Premier League, I could leave home much later than usual on a Saturday if I was working at the Amex Stadium, and I was able to tell the inside story of the Albion's promotion, which appeared as the book *Brighton Up*.

Many football fans envy the job of football writer, and rightly so. Being paid to attend games and report matches feels like a lottery win every week. But the downside is that you don't often get to pick and choose your destinations. So although I was lucky enough to be able to report on Brighton's Premier League debut at home to Manchester City, their first win (against West Bromwich Albion), their first away win (at West Ham) and their first victory over one of the big clubs (at home to Arsenal), I was in press boxes elsewhere when they faced Liverpool, went to Chelsea, and thrashed Swansea City 4-1.

Kevin Clarke saw all those games and more. He was one of those supporters for whom 19 home matches against the elite of English football was not enough. They wanted to be there as the team played on the great stages that many had only ever seen on TV - Anfield, Old Trafford, The Emirates, Wembley. Kevin set out to do the lot: all 19 away games, from Newcastle to Bournemouth to Swansea, taking his son Jacob along for some memorable rides.

I have been to all those grounds, of course, but never in a single season and seldom to see the Albion. 'Away' shows what I was missing. It's not often that you feel jealous of someone taking a trip to Stoke …

Brighton, October 2018

Nick Szczepanik

Freelance sports writer and author

Acknowledgements

Foreword

Are you a football fan? Are you a **true** football fan?

Having a team isn't enough....

Do you feel physical gut wrenching pain when your team loses?

Does a last minute winning goal render you incapable of controlling body and mind as you spiral into an ecstasy normally only reserved for carnal pleasure or substance abuse?

Do you go AWAY...?

1. The Kick-off

The Holy Grail for a true football fan is, at some point in their life, to do the full season, home and away – all 38 or 46 league games. You may only ever do it once. Noel Gallagher still reflects on his as one of the life achievements that he is most proud of, with Manchester City in the pre-billionaire years.

I've just (almost) done it with Brighton and Hove Albion Football Club, in their first season in the Premier League (37 out of 38 games – damn that US work trip and the rescheduling of Spurs at home!) I'm glad I went for it; it takes dedication, effort, money, time and – above all else – the sales skills of The Wolf of Wall Street to convince your other half! But this book isn't about that: it's about the 19 away games that I did with my 17-year-old son, Jacob.

Because football is more than the game and the results. It allows fathers and sons to share an experience that isn't age-dependent and can have the longevity of a marriage with all the ups and downs that go with that. Hmm: in this day and age that sounds a bit sexist, doesn't it? I can sense my daughter, Megan, holding me to account: 'What about mothers and daughters, eh, Dad?'

On reflection, I'm not apologising. It's different and it's not sexist. Men struggle more than women to open up, talk and to be physically affectionate. Football doesn't solve all that, but it helps.

And do you know what? There is something inherently traditional and touching about a father and son going to football: the images it conjures in the mind, from holding the hand of your son as you take him to his first game, all the way through to him helping you to get up the stairs and into your seat as the generations pass. I love it – sorry, Megan x.

1

It truly is quality time (God, what a shit phrase that is). It is *real* time with your son, travelling together, eating together, experiencing the pre-game excitement, predictions and endless chats about players, formations and tactics. 'Oh yeah, the five at the back becomes three when we attack; we all have to press together; the game management needs to improve; we are not keeping our shape; I prefer us with three Number 10s and no striker.' I can do them all, endlessly. That, coupled with the shared depression, disbelief and injustice of a defeat, wallowing in an all-encompassing silence, occasionally peppered with a random observation, usually followed by an expletive.

Father and son together from August to May: yep, that is a real commitment, certainly the longest that my son Jacob has made in his 17 short years. Will he ever make a bigger one? How do you explain that? It's simple – you can't. As Jacob said, 'You just don't get it, Mum.' That boy is ahead of his time. He will become one of the world's great orators with that level of simplicity and impact!

So, how do I capture this experience? How is it relevant to anyone else but me and maybe Jacob, if he can be bothered to read it? (To set expectations, when Twitter doubled its character limit from 140 to 280, it was a stretch for him.)

I could have a chapter on each game: 19 chapters, how very organised – I am a bit OCD so that could work for me (I could do it alphabetically as well – stop it now Kevin...). But if I put myself in your shoes, it could get just a touch repetitive: like a George Graham Arsenal performance without the one goal (if there is anyone under 40 reading this, I just lost them).

Equally, capturing all the results as we go along, with Brighton's league position, as the season develops and we reach a crescendo at the end, would be of mild interest to a Brighton fan, stattos and the anoraks out there (there is a bit of that in me, but I hide it well), but for everyone else? Mmmmm...boring.

So, what have I done? Well I have attempted to bring to life the whole experience of the 19 away games. You see, the football is just part of it. I don't think that non-football fans get that, and it's emphasised 100 times over when you go away. I want this book to resonate with you football fans reading this, whatever category you fall into, from season ticket holder to occasional *Match of the Day* watcher. But I also want to explain to the non-footy fans; I would like you to come away from reading this book with at least an understanding of not only what we do but why we keep coming back for more, the addiction – even if you choose never to inhale this particular drug.

Bear in mind that a typical away trip could be anything from a couple of hours down the road to Crystal Palace or Southampton, up to six hours each way for Newcastle, and maybe an overnight stay to throw into the mix. The football is only 90-95 minutes. The rest of this experience could be anything from eight hours to a day and a half!

This book tries to capture the whole thing: the match and what is going on in the rest of that time. It's who you meet, it's where you have been and the impact on family life. It's how something that can start out so mundane on the face of it can take a turn into a hilarious moment, often involving complete strangers, that becomes an anecdote that you will now churn out for 30 years plus.

It's the people watching. The pensioners with a Ready Brek glow about them of stories past, glory days and tragedies in equal measure. The anoraks who can recall every statistic you could imagine, some appearing barely to exist outside of their football experience, suddenly coming alive at a game. The funny, the deluded, the drunk, the depressed, the nutters, the early leavers, the half-and-half scarf wearers (yuk!) and of course the eternal optimists.

All a complete mix of society, from every background you could imagine, different ages, appearances, rich, poor and in-between with often nothing else in common but their love of Brighton & Hove Albion.

With the away fans, though, it's all magnified that bit more - like one of those old newsreels or movies being digitally re mastered from black and white into glorious technicolour. Their love is deeper, their passion stronger, which results in them travelling all over the country, spending vast amounts of money to get their Brighton fix. This is all epitomised by the standing and the singing. When you are away, you stand for the entire game and you sing non-stop. That never happens at a home game, not even against Palace.

You see, it's different away. Everyone should do it at least once, footy fan or not...

I have to be honest with you as well, reader. Maybe, just maybe, this book is one for me. I always wanted to write one, with some random interest from family and friends (the loyal ones or the patronising ones; it doesn't matter which category you are in). If that's the case, I can deal with that. I'm happy with that, so let's do it.

For everyone else, give it a go. If it fills a gap on a train, a park bench, in bed, on the beach (you get the picture) then great. If it ends up as something to put your coffee on, or feed to the log burner (how middle class) or wipe your arse with (how coarse), then so be it. Now let's begin...

2. The Epiphany

Saturday August 19th 2017; Jacob and I were preparing to leave for Brighton's first ever away Premier League fixture, against Leicester City.

The previous week we had watched Brighton play their first ever Premier League game, at our home, the Amex Stadium, where we experienced a respectable 2-0 loss against Manchester City, the champions-to-be. City are owned by billionaire sheiks and managed by Pep Guardiola, widely thought of as the best coach in the world, and have a team assembled at a cost of hundreds of millions of pounds. That said, it was a good time to play them, right at the start of the season before their footballing rhythm and beauty was in full flow. And it also has to be said that we looked bloody nervous!

It felt like we had got away with one. Now we went on to face the side who, in one of the greatest shocks in sporting history, had won the league title in 2015-16 - as their fans reminded us on arrival at the King Power Stadium. In the summer sunshine before the kick off, they belted out at the top of their voices: "You'll never sing that, you'll never sing that, Premier League champions, you'll never sing that!"

As with all good football songs, succinct, to the point and repeated multiple times!

We were now getting very excited: a packed stadium, and more importantly a full away end, whose numbers were slightly reduced after a couple of ejections by the stewards. One offender was about my age and should have known better, and another about Jacob's age, a football hooligan wannabe.

The noise from both sets of supporters was vibrating round the ground. We had great seats (although we were standing of course), and as the stadium announcer bellowed out the players' names from both sides, I could feel goose bumps. Then 52 seconds later Leicester scored.

Suddenly the pre-game excitement of the car journey, the walk into the ground with around two and a half thousand other Brighton fans singing joyously, the chats with mates, the nods to acquaintances, the smiles wherever you looked, were all forgotten after this dose of reality. Shit, this is going to be a tough season; do we have a hope of staying up?

It was still 1-0 at half time. We were still in it, our hearts told us; our heads said we had lots of new signings that needed bedding in and it showed.

Nine minutes into the second half and a young man whom Leicester had signed from Hull, who was man of the match so far - simultaneously a rock in defence, whilst carrying the ball effortlessly out from the back and who would become an England World Cup star of the future - smashed a bullet header into the top corner. The unicorn racing Harry Maguire had arrived.

After that it was *really a routine win for Leicester, but even so our appetite had been whetted. We wanted more of this;* the placebo of *Match of the Day* would not be enough.

Then followed Watford, where we secured our first away point with a 0-0 draw. We should have won as, encouragingly, at last we played the football we were capable of. But we couldn't round it off with a goal and there was still a nagging doubt as Watford has been reduced to ten men after only 24 minutes due to a horror tackle by their defender Miguel Britos on Brighton winger Anthony Knockaert. Alan Shearer and Gary Lineker were suitably horrified, but at least

Knockaert somehow came out of it still able to not only walk but finish the game.

Our first Premier League win finally happened at the fourth attempt, 3-1 at home to West Bromwich Albion, with two goals from Pascal Gross, who would turn out to be the bargain of the season at £3 million from Ingolstadt. However, this book is entitled Away, so as good as it was, I'm not dwelling on that victory here.

We went on to Bournemouth away with renewed hope, and took the lead before snatching defeat from the jaws of victory. Jordon Ibe came on for them as a substitute and changed the game: 2-1 to Bournemouth - ouch!

Then came a 1-0 home win against Newcastle and a 2-0 defeat away to Arsenal, notable only for how quiet the Arsenal fans were (the famous Highbury library had clearly moved unaltered into the Emirates Stadium) and a 25-yard Solly March screamer that hit the post - it could all have been so different, we told ourselves.

Next was a heart breaking 1-1 draw at home to Everton, when Wayne Rooney, showing all the early-season form that would lead him to move to Major League Soccer in the United States at the end of the season, equalised against the run of play in the dying minutes, converting a penalty after our legendary captain, Bruno, had an uncharacteristic moment of poor judgement and elbowed Everton's teenage striker Dominic Calvert-Lewin in the face - arghhhh!!! (On all levels!)

Before you ask; yes, I do realise that I'm just rattling off games and results now, which I promised I wouldn't do. But there is a method to my madness as this all led to West Ham away on a Friday night at the end of October, which I will talk about for different reasons later in the book.

I made the executive call that, based on a Friday night 8pm kick off in London, I didn't want the grief of getting home and it would be nice to have a bite to eat and a few beers with Jacob. So the Travelodge it was - it's always glamorous with me, I can tell you!

This was the night of the game changer, and it happened before the match. It clearly wasn't our run of away results that had prompted it, as you can see from the previous couple of paragraphs: four away games, three defeats and a draw; one point gained and only one goal scored, so why did I have this epiphany?

What did it for me was that I was having such a great time with my son. Of course, a win would be the icing on the cake, or a goal even! But it was the experience, the away trips, our time together and the realisation that Jacob was 17. There was no doubt in my mind that this was the last opportunity to do this. He would be 18 next season, drinking (legally) and going with his mates. So I popped the question like a nervous boyfriend preparing his marriage proposal.

"What do ya reckon, Jacob? About doing all 19 away games? It's our first season in the Premier League, our last chance before you are off with your mates. It's something we would only ever do once in our lives. It's a bucket list moment."

I was now going into full sales mode.

"We may never get in the Premier League again. We may only have one season; we may go down. Think of the grounds you haven't been to, like Old Trafford, Goodison Park and Spurs at Wembley".

I paused for breath...

"Yeah, all right," he muttered, barely audible.

WE WERE ON!!!

3. Henry & Uncle Dan

The season was now in full flow and Jacob and I were on a roll. Since that decision had been made to go for the 100 percent away attendance we hadn't looked back. I was surprised, pleased and proud that Jacob had stepped up to the plate and was not only showing some drive and commitment, but also appeared to be enjoying himself (it can be hard to tell sometimes).

I was acutely aware that there are always other things that teenagers could be doing; like lying in bed, binge eating, sleeping bordering on hibernating, attempting to complete a whole sentence without losing interest and inclination half way through, getting a haircut (these appear to be required almost weekly), flooding the bathroom, asking for money and in general just existing in a permanent state of being laid-back.

So, this burst of teenage energy driven by our mission was welcome, more than welcome. I was loving this opportunity that had presented itself unexpectedly. The laughs, jokes, embarrassing dad moments, piss-taking and dissecting of the Brighton team were all brilliant, but the best bit was going with my mate, who happened to be my son.

This was an irreplaceable and unique moment in our lives. Yes, I know what I just said and trust me, I'm not over stating it. Normally when moments like this happen in life you are not necessarily cognisant of it at the time. The impact happens when you reflect on great occasions spent with family and friends. But, I was very aware right from the moment when Jacob muttered "Yeah, all right" to my proposal. This enabled me to be conscious of what we were doing, and, importantly, mindful enough of that to savour the special moments as they happened - so many crammed into one football season and 19 trips around the country.

Where else and how else could you engineer that amount of one-on-one time with your teenage son? (That was a rhetorical question, but feel free to ponder it for a moment.) Football, you see, non-believers - there is more to it than you might think...

But all that said, occasionally we had a guest appearance on an away trip. Our first of the season was Henry, Jacobs's mate, who joined us for Bournemouth and Huddersfield, both defeats I might add. Now footballers may be superstitious, but we fans are even worse. I decided after Huddersfield that as nice as Henry was, he would need to be making his own way to any future games.

You have to be ruthless, take the emotion out of it, it's a results business, and sometimes you have to sacrifice the niceties, take one for the team so those magical three points can be secured. Henry's exit, although sad, could be a turning point. Maybe my brother-in-law, Dan, will bring us the boost we need away at Chelsea. More of that later.

Back to Henry. His main contribution was that he exploded the myth of the teenager. After meeting Henry, it became clear that Jacob had been grooming me for the previous few months of the season. All I could expect from Jacob on the car journey was a chat for the first 20 minutes on a bad day, maybe up to an hour on a good one, then it was sleep time until he was awoken (sometimes) by the car being parked. The lack of motion could stir him out of his deep slumber, no doubt dreaming of one of the Kardashians or maybe picturing himself as one of those Grime artists (with the Kardashians) or scoring the winner for the Albion.

Then he would get out of the car in a kind of extra-slow motion, entering the service station almost frame by frame (an x2 opposed to an x30 on your Live TV forward button, so to speak). When he was fed and watered, the colour would return to his cheeks, the deadness of his eyes would start to transform from the look of a great white shark - a sleepy version - into a playful puppy, sometimes humour, a smile and even laughter. Then, just after hitting his peak, his energy bar would start to dwindle like a video game fighter who has taken too many punches. And finally, his light would be extinguished as he re-joined the world of Stormzy, Kim K & Glenn Murray, leaving me alone with a cappuccino, a chicken Caesar wrap and talkSPORT.

But Henry was different. He started chatting away as soon as he got in the car (well, these teenagers always peak early), he was knowledgeable and funny, eruditely moving from topic to topic. Football, college, family, current affairs – then I noticed the time: it had been two hours, then three. What was going on? This wasn't how it worked.

I had long since forgiven him for being a Chelsea fan, which is unheard of for me, even though I should have been one (sorry Grandad – a topic for later). I looked for signs of weariness, but he was still pressing on. I toggled between being grateful to Henry for making the journey time feel like we had done it in a Ferrari rather than an X1, and glancing at my sleeping son, feeling betrayed at how he had played me so easily. Bastard!

Our journey ventured ever closer to the holy grail of Huddersfield and the six-pointer. There are so many six-pointers now aren't there? It's hardly worth turning up for three points these days. It's like 'Super Sunday.' I feel short-changed when it's just ... well, just 'Sunday.' That's reserved for something like Stoke versus West Bromwich Albion. That could be 'Superfluous Sunday', 'Sanguine Sunday' or maybe just a 'Shit Sunday'.

Anyway, Henry, my cultured guest, told me that he had never been this far North before, really. 'You've never been up North before?' I enquired.

'Yes.' he replied. 'Birmingham.'

Just when I thought this trip couldn't get any better, it had now become a rite of passage for Henry! When, on arrival, he fully integrated into his surroundings by ordering chips and gravy, I could almost hear the angels singing as if in the climax to one of those religious epics. Suddenly Henry took on the look of a young Charlton Heston – pre his campaign on the Second Amendment, supporting the right for every American to keep and bear arms!

'Uncle Dan' was our second guest. He is actually my brother-in-law, but I have got into an unbreakable routine of referring to him as 'Uncle Dan.' That's what having kids does to you. He is a favourite with my children, although they wouldn't necessarily admit that to him. Sorry Megan, Jacob and Fin. I have blown your cover!

I have known Dan since he was 11 or 12. He is now heading towards 40, which I think is alarming for both of us for different reasons. We have a lot of football history together: I took him to his first match to see Nott's County at Meadow Lane against Peterborough: it's always important not to set the benchmark too high at the beginning.

He had started out down the more traditional route in Nottingham of being a Forest fan. A couple of European Cups & the Brian Clough effect tend to steer the locals in this direction.

But then he had a lightning-bolt moment. One of his school teachers, whom he was particularly fond of, was a big County fan. Dan was drawn into his stories and recollections and before you know it he had consigned himself to a lifetime of football misery

12

supporting a club whose two main claims to fame are: being the oldest club in the league (fair enough); and being the inspiration behind Juventus playing in black and white stripes (true – but not exactly up there in terms of footballing credentials).

So, during Dan's formative years, whenever he visited us in London along with his younger sister, I took it upon myself to educate him in the world of football beyond County, taking him to various games across London.

Highlights included Selhurst Park in November 1994, where Wimbledon played Newcastle. At the time this game broke the record for the most attempts on goal in the Premier League. An incredible match, it ended 3-2, lit up by Peter Beardsley's magic and the inevitable sending off for Vinnie Jones. I think his tackle would have warranted three straight reds, community service and a feature-length edition of *Panorama* by current standards. Even Graeme Souness would have winced. Hmm, on reflection maybe not.

Spurs versus Leeds ended 3-3. Sol Campbell scored a late equaliser under the stewardship of ex Gunners player and manager George Graham, who had also managed Leeds. We were sat with the Spurs fans, but with only a painfully thin-looking orange line of stewards between us and the Leeds boys who seemed even more aggressive than normal – all part of the education, Dan! There was however a touching point of consensus between the supporters in relation to their mutual hatred of the aforementioned Mr Graham.

Then there was the Subbuteo ground that is QPR's Loftus Road, where Ray Wilkins, aged about 58, gave an unbelievable display in midfield for the Hoops. I swear he didn't leave the centre circle for 90 minutes but managed to run the game spraying passes left and right, and forward, against all those preconceptions of him being a bit of a crab like midfielder. All whilst the floodlights glowed off his perfectly round bald head, giving him a movie star quality – Yul Brynner-like in *The King & I*; he beckoned to the opposing midfielders: 'Shall we dance?'

Strangely, from all these memories, the recollection that we talk about most was linked to gambling rather than football. It was at Stamford Bridge, where a Ruud Gullit-managed Chelsea team including Gianluca Vialli up front took to the pitch. The tickets were particularly expensive – typical Chelsea, eh? Even pre Abramovich – so I thought now was the right moment to introduce Dan to the beauty of the football bet.

I eased him in gently with the first goal scorer option for a quid. I boldly selected Frank Le Beouf, the French Chelsea centre half, future World Cup winner – not that he ever mentions that, of course! – And an actor, in essence like Cantona with a charisma by pass, at 33-1. I can't remember how much I put on. Except that it wasn't a lot. But what I do remember is discussing with Dan that if this bet came off, it would pay for the tickets and then some.

Well you now know what's coming. Frank rose like a salmon to deliver an instant deposit into my bank account. Dan still talks of the infringement that he spotted in the build up to the goal. I was too busy just watching Frank like a hawk at the time and then going into raptures of celebration, never done before or since for a Chelsea goal. It should have been disallowed, he told me. What a load of bollocks, what does this 12 year old know?

Match of the Day proved him right. He never lets me forget that and the fact that he was the only person in the ground to spot it. All I can say is thank God that Ladbrokes don't run a retrospective panel to review the validity of their first goal scorer bets. I'm also slightly relieved that after witnessing my glory, the celebrations and the 'free' tickets, that Dan didn't end up in The Priory for some kind of teenage gambling addiction.

I have digressed I admit, but what a smooth link back to Stamford Bridge where Dan was our guest for Chelsea v Brighton on Boxing Day. Well, I wish I had an inspiring story to tell about a day packed with incident, but it wasn't quite like that. Dan had to sit in the home end, which was the only way we could get a ticket, courtesy of my Chelsea supporting mate, Sid – a lovely fella who has a nose somewhere between Barry Manilow, Gru from *Despicable Me*, and Karl Malden (look him up – *The Streets of San Francisco* is a clue). Put it this way, if you had a cocaine habit you wouldn't want to be sharing with Sid. Not that he has one, by the way. Two bitter shandies and a Bailey's chaser and he is finished. I'm deadly serious, and yes, that is what he drinks!

In summary, a functional 2-0 win for Chelsea, expensive coffee and a nightmare finding somewhere to park (God, I'm so middle aged). But there was also one moment of angst/moral code/political correctness.

When we took our seats in the away end, plastered on the back of each one in capital letters was an instruction to REMAIN SEATED.

Any away fan knows that you stand for the entire game, singing relentlessly, like a throwback to days gone by. That's a huge part of the attractiveness of the event, and why else would you go to Stoke or Huddersfield?

I assumed this was just Chelsea being a touch heavy handed. They are not known for their subtlety. This is the club, after all, where Ken Bates, the then chairman, wanted to put up 12 foot electric fences to keep the supporters under control as a result of the hooligan era of the late 70s and early 80s. The Greater London Council [GLC] under the leadership of future London Mayor and Brent East MP Ken Livingstone, declined Mr Bates's request, which was a good job as he would probably have presided over more executions than George W Bush as Governor of Texas – for the record, about one every nine days whilst he was in office.

Then I realised why we had the Remain Seated sign as I looked behind me and saw that the wheelchair area, normally close to the pitch or raised for an unobstructed view, was actually behind our seats. If I'm honest, with shame I have to recollect that my heart sank: I've come here to stand, not to sit down, what were the club thinking? And how dare they place this moral dilemma on my shoulders? Stand, as is the right of the away fan, or sit down to keep the view clear for the supporters in the wheelchairs? I didn't sign up for this. 90 minutes of parking the bus with the odd break way attack and the lamenting of the late use of substitutes, that's what I was here for.

There was a lot of pre-match discussion that I listened into intently. It was marginally more entertaining than the pre-game announcer on the pitch who had clearly not bothered to do his research on the pronunciation of the Brighton players' surnames. As a result he was drowned out by the chants of 'You don't know what you're doing' normally reserved for the ref. The consensus was that this obstructed view was not fair on the supporters in the wheelchairs. One guy even called the stewards over to outline his concerns in quite granular detail.

Once the whistle blew at 3pm for kick off, everyone stood up as one and all previous concerns seemed to slip away as the football became more important, which was not a proud moment. Mr 'Granular' did make a point of speaking to the stewards again at half time. But, however strongly he felt about this injustice, all I can say is that he didn't feel the need to sit down or move in the second half. His principles did not inspire him to the point of actually taking some action. Rosa Parks he was not, but then I'm hardly speaking from a position of strength.

It did take me back to another wheelchair-related incident where it's fair to say I didn't cover myself in glory. Through work I was hosted by a supplier at a Hall of Fame dinner in Liverpool, along with a colleague of mine. The evening was also a special tribute to the Liverpool 1977 European Cup-winning team, many of whose players were in attendance.

My colleague, Andy, was a scouser and big Liverpool fan, but was shy and feeling slightly intimidated about approaching some of the ex-players as they were childhood heroes for him. I decided to take responsibility and get him introduced to every single one that I could lay my eyes on. This resulted in a very entertaining evening as I got braver and braver as the beer flowed.

My alcohol-induced courage resulted in many chats with the Reds legends along with Andy, who was loving it. Phil Thompson shared with us his story of how as captain he was in possession of the European Cup on the plane home and then took it down his local pub, Alan Kennedy walked us through his two European Cup final-winning goals and Phil Neal, the most decorated player in the game pre-Ryan Giggs, shared his Liverpool and England memories including coaching Paul Gascoigne. I was on a roll.

Then I spotted him: the ultimate Liverpool legend, the godfather of the club, Kenny Dalglish. Voted their best player of all time, he also managed them to their most recent league title win back in 1990. I turned to Andy, gave him the camera and marched off to secure a picture of us with Kenny. As if to confirm his legendary status, there was a queue to have a photo with him, unlike Neal, Kennedy and Thompson who seemed pleased that anyone would want to hear their stories.

I waited patiently and, finally, there he was in front of me. I introduced myself and Andy, thrust our camera into a stranger's hands and asked him to take the picture, job done. I put my arm round Andy as we walked away; there was no topping this one. Then I took a look at the picture and felt mildly nauseous: it was blurred! I couldn't believe it.

Andy said: 'Never mind mate, never mind!' But we couldn't get this close and then fail. I charged back to Kenny, bundling people out of my way, straight to the front of the line. 'Kenny, Kenny, sorry mate,' I slurred slightly, 'the picture's blurred. Can we have another one, mate?'

I plonked myself next to Kenny and stood proudly, thrusting the camera back into the stranger's hands. Kenny was just looking at me, not the camera, like a rabbit in the headlights, staring. The guy with the camera had a look of mild disgust on his face.

Then I realised that Andy hadn't joined us. My eyes met his and I saw him looking at me, slightly panicked, and gesturing for me to look downwards.

And there he was, Kenny Dalglish biography in his hands, holding out a pen for a signature, a guy in a wheelchair – whom I had just not only pushed in front of, but stood in front of whilst he was in the middle of his intro to Kenny, my backside now in his face.

What can I say? I'm 6' 6'and he was out of my peripheral vision. I apologised quickly and took my camera back. The look of mild disgust from the stranger had moved on to outright disdain. He handed the camera back to me as if it was riddled with a deadly disease that he would catch if he held onto it for a moment longer. I exited the scene swiftly, being sure not to catch the eye of anyone in the surrounding area, which was the start of my problem.

No more photos that night. They say things come in threes, don't they? Suffice to say that whenever I see someone in a wheelchair now, I break out in a cold sweat, fearing an impending catastrophe of my own making. An *Ironside* re-run on ITV3 can leave me shaking as I desperately fumble with the remote to prevent Raymond Burr from eyeballing me any longer with his disapproving stare.

4. Smethwick, Stoke & satnavs

My football routine has changed significantly since becoming a father. In my childless days the process was very simple: get on a train, find the local pub, get in there early doors to get a spot and drink copious amounts of lager before entering the ground, where the biggest challenge then became the timing of your trips to the gents to offload the aforementioned lager whilst ensuring that you didn't miss any key pivotal moments during the game – commonly known as goals.

But as a dad there is much more responsibility: no booze as you will most likely be driving, and of course you are now a role model! Although I have made it clear to Jacob that once the game starts, I accept no responsibility for my actions. Various stops are required, mainly for food and of course now being in possession of a vehicle, you have the dreaded football parking challenge.

Can I park near the ground? How much will it cost? Will there be any spaces left? What time do I need to get there? Should I park further away to avoid the inevitable gridlock after the game, when people take over the roads and peer at the drivers with that look that says 'Why the hell did you park this close to the ground?', turning to their mates to shake their heads in disbelief and utter the word 'prick.'

But now in this age of technology, we have apps for everything: music, banking, holidays, our football teams and now, of course, parking – yeah!

What a great idea – you can pay to park on somebody's drive, all done on the app, paid up front and your space is guaranteed. I have bored my friends with this when they make the mistake of asking me where I parked. I'm so down with the technology man.

Weird, isn't it, the male obsession with parking and in particular directions? 'Yeah mate, what you wanna do is take the A24, cut down that left by McDonalds – you know, near the Shell garage – over two mini roundabouts, bear left, past that lamp post with the white dog shit next to it, left at the house with the swingers' pampas grass outside, right where that paving slab is slightly ajar, then pull over on the right next to the Monster Munch crisp packet that I embedded into the wall when I last went there 20 years ago, *Shawshank Redemption*-style!'

I have never been a typical bloke in this sense for one very good reason: I struggle to find my way to the end of my street without the assistance of a satnav. I know it's a terrible admission: it's like saying I suffer from erectile dysfunction or I can't put up a shelf, or wire a plug or down a pint in one. For clarity, all of those apply to me except one. I will leave you to decide – answers on a postcard, send a stamped addressed envelope if you want a response.

In fact, even when someone starts to give me directions, I just switch off after about the second sentence. I'm not sure if it's boredom, or maybe that part of my brain that should compute this stuff just died, probably of boredom. Needless to say the satnav is my saviour, a wonder of the world, up there with the pyramids, the Hanging Gardens of Babylon and Bobby Zamora.

But where parking is concerned, with my app I'm more than happy to engage in the conversation. It's taken all that pre game angst away. What could be simpler?

Or so you would think. I have two examples this season that took me down a somewhat unexpected route into a series of unfortunate events. Who would have thought that parking could be such a potentially dangerous activity?

West Brom away – parking secured in Smethwick via the app. Oh yes, I'm on top of my game. The satnav had taken me into a small council estate. There was my spot, a bit tight but I can get in. So, all done, I'm now putting on my 15 layers of clothing, which has become essential in my advancing years as I seem to have no resistance to cold weather whatsoever. The temperature dropping is like the kryptonite effect on Superman; I wilt and groan until I'm finally rendered incapable of speech or movement.

Due to my incapacity, I sort of stand there with my arms and the top half of my body in a fixed position; turning around involves the full use of my entire body to do a 360-degree rotation. The upside is that if I was ever attacked by the opposing fans, they could kick me around for hours and I wouldn't feel a thing, even a knife would be rendered useless as it would only penetrate around 50% of my clothed layers at worst. Although the flaw in that argument is a head shot, a bit like the perils of the bullet proof vest. Maybe I will start wearing a crash helmet as well?

So there I am outside the car, putting up with Jacob's heavy sighing at having to wait sooooo long for me. Then I hear a voice and look up. There is an elderly Asian man hanging out the window of his bathroom upstairs telling me in a very animated way that I can't park there and that I will be clamped. I'm struggling to understand him.

Is this starting to sound racist? Or is that just the heightened sensitivity I have to that now courtesy of my daughter and her boyfriend who are trying to educate the old man in these new very politically correct times? I didn't think I needed any help; I've always been well balanced and non-judgemental around gender, colour et cetera, or so I thought.

But then, when watching a movie with said daughter and boyfriend, I mentioned that one of the main actors reminded me of 50 cent, the rapper. Megan's boyfriend responded by saying: 'Yeah, you're right and that's not even racist because he does actually look like him.' What the fuck, I feel this dialogue says it all and requires no further commentary. Hopefully you can see why I'm a bit self-analytical on this subject now.

Back to my new friend hanging out the window. I'm now struggling to compute what's going on, like the effect of getting directions! He is saying I can't park here, I am saying I've paid for the space, he is saying I can't park here and I WILL get clamped, I am saying ... oh, you get the picture.

Then suddenly it dawned on me: there is a third party involved in this. He is right, I am right, which only leaves the satnav. God forbid that it has taken me to the wrong address. I shuddered at just the thought of this impossibility. The very foundation of my being was shaken. I walked slowly back to the car, feeling as if the temperature had dropped another couple of degrees (note to self I think I have an extra body warmer in the boot).

I looked at my sat nav, I looked at the road sign, I looked at the sat nav, I looked at the road sign, I looked at the sat nav, I looked at the road sign, I looked at Jacob. His expression gave off a certain vibe that I can only describe as 'For fuck's sake, Dad'. I looked at Jacob, then back at the road sign, then at the man at the window. He was still repeating the same words (I think).

I now felt like I was swimming under water. It was surreal – can the satnav really be wrong? Then it dawned on me, the realisation, it wasn't the satnav after all. I had put the wrong address into it.

Relief swept over me. My faith in satnavs was restored. I would have to take a long hard look at myself, however. I took a moment to contemplate that, then got back in the car quickly, or as quickly as was possible with 15 layers on, and drove off in desperate search of the correct address.

I felt like I was about to spontaneously combust, driving round the streets of Smethwick. There's a TV series in that I'm sure, with Frank Skinner and Adrian Chiles as the two fumbling Midlands cops banging up the wrong people, but in a humorous way. Sweating profusely, I kept saying to myself: 'I should have taken my coats off first (plural is correct by the way). Where is this place?'

Then we turned into a new-build estate and I became immediately aware that everyone was staring at me and Jacob as if to say: 'You shouldn't be here.' Had we inadvertently displayed some reference to Brighton & Hove Albion Football Club on our clothing or in the car, I thought?

Can't be, I have never been one for colours at a game. Why do grown men feel the need to wear football kits to matches? It's worse in the modern age as well, as middle aged men with bellies that, as one of my mates would say, are 'all bought and paid for' try to crow bar themselves into the skin-tight modern shirts built for Premier League stars with a zero-percent body fat rating. These tops are completely unforgiving, highlighting any minor physical imperfection. In the worst cases they roll up and become a kind of old man's crop top. Maybe in the future it will catch on to have a belly button piercing with your club badge on display.

There is also a parental responsibility here. When I see one of those kids turning up to a game with the full kit on including shorts and socks as well – or as in one case I saw; a lad with all that plus shin pads – then I'm afraid I have to look at the dad. What kind of role model are you? How did you let him out of the house like that? Almost as embarrassing as the half-and-half scarf, made for football tourists who have no concept of that fact that football is built around rivalry and tribalism.

Back to the car, then it dawned on me: the message behind the stares was basically translated as: 'I hope they don't think they are going to park round here!'

Initially two guys waved to get my attention: 'Where you going, mate? You can't park here.' I explained that I had paid to park on someone's drive. Blimey, it's so simple to explain the beauty of this system down at the pub. But when doing the same to complete strangers whose opening stance is 'You ain't parking here, mate', suddenly it's a tad more difficult. I started to question why I had used this poxy app in the first place.

Then a guy in a white estate drove past us, then circled round us, then passed us again, his stare unwavering as he parked opposite our spot. 'What you doing? You can't park there, mate.' Groundhog Day ensued as I explained AGAIN. 'I know,' I thought, 'I can close this argument down simply. I will just knock on the door of the house of where I have parked and they can explain.' Why hadn't I thought of this earlier?

I knocked, turned, smiled at the guy in the white estate. His facial expression and stare hadn't changed for about 10 minutes now. I knocked again and rang the doorbell. I could feel his eyes burning into my soul. I peered in the window and then it hit me – they were not in. Aarghhh!

I looked behind for Jacob; for some moral support. Where was he? Still in the bloody car on his phone completely oblivious to my problems. Typical. I'm surprised he hadn't fallen asleep: teenage narcolepsy is more common that you might think, especially in 17-year-olds from the south coast of England called Jacob.

Right, that's it – my patience had gone. Come on, Jacob; let's go. I walked past the man in the car, defiant. Then just as I thought it was all over and we were off the estate, on the main road, walking towards the ground, suddenly out of nowhere I could hear shouting and this guy was running towards us from the estate shouting at the top of his voice 'You can't park there – you can't park there.'

I was at the end of my tether. Could I explain it all again? The app, the fact I had paid to park there, I couldn't help it that the guy wasn't in to corroborate my story. Then I had an out-of-body experience, like those ones that people have when they die on the operating table and are hovering over their own body watching themselves. It was happening to me and I heard my other self say: 'Fuck off mate, I'll park where I like!'

The epilogue to this story is that West Brom, who hadn't won for 19 games, beat us 2-0 and it could have been more. I've had better days at the office.

Bad Parking Experience 2, Stoke away, a movie title if ever I heard one: the sequel to Bad Parking Experience, starring a young-looking George Clooney, with his son played by Benny from Crossroads. Jacob won't have a clue on this reference. Google it, son.

I had stepped up my interaction with the parking app on this one. I actually engaged in text dialogue directly with the owner of the house where we were parking, to confirm the walking distance to the ground. The Google view on the route was that her estimation would require me to have the speed and stamina of an Olympic gold medallist to do it in the 20 mins stipulated. The alarm bells should have started ringing right there and then.

I've always prided myself on being an excellent judge of character. Years in sales have helped me to hone that skill down to a fine art. But we can all have an off day, can't we? And, to be fair, I hadn't actually met her, and was destined never to do so, as it turned out. One day we will sit down and laugh together about how these events progressed, but not yet and, to be honest, I doubt I will ever go back to Stoke.

So, I've followed the parking instructions to the letter. It's a bunch of flats with a car park out the back, under an archway, drive straight ahead and in, no other cars present as we arrived. We left and headed off on the slightly elongated walk to the ground. I was in good spirits, so was prepared to give her the benefit of the doubt.

Fast forward to the end of the game. What a match, by the way. At first we looked very comfortable for a victory and three points after a sensational goal from José Izquierdo. It followed some good passing which culminated in a series of one-twos and a composed finish from Izzy. We were in raptures: the best goal we had seen Brighton score this season (since Izzy's last one at the Amex) and it was against one of our relegation rivals.

As an aside, the joy turned to frustration and annoyance with *Match of the Day* that night; I got ready to bask in the glory of that goal and all the praise that Gary Lineker and company would lavish on the team and Izquierdo for this Barcelona-esque goal that Pep Guardiola and Lionel Messi would have been proud of at their peak. Only to discover in utter disbelief that they were moving on to the next game and they hadn't even deemed it worthy of a replay, let alone comment. You see, BBC, this is why BT Sport & Sky are taking over: poor, very poor; the smaller clubs again treated differently. Let's be honest, if the goal had involved Kane, De Bruyne or Salah, they would have purred over it for 10 minutes, but oh no, not for the Seagulls!

So, back to being one up. Then Stoke's only world-class player, Xherdan Shaqiri ('the Alpine Messi,' as I'm reliably told the Swiss call him) knocked one in from outside the box. 1-1 and suddenly the game changed out of all recognition and we were now far from comfortable.

It culminated in an amazing and highly comical (as it turned out) finish. Stoke were awarded a very dubious penalty for an alleged push by Dale Stephens, so dubious in fact that not even the Stoke players claimed for it. The *Match of the Day* panel also concurred, to try and regain some credibility no doubt.

What followed was like being back in the playground or over in the park with your mates, as seasoned pro (and just on as a substitute) Charlie Adam went running after the ball, hurdling the advertising boards on the way in his desperation to get there first so he could take the penalty.

Meanwhile Stoke's new signing, the aptly-named Jesé, who had won this outrageously soft penalty, had other ideas and was trying to wrestle the ball from Adam's grasp. Suddenly all the Stoke players were involved in trying to resolve the situation as their manager Paul Lambert looked on, perplexed.

The hurdling of the advertising boards having given him the edge, Adam stepped up to take the kick, ready now to take his moment of glory by scoring the winning goal in injury time, securing Stoke a much needed three points after coming from behind against their relegation rivals The script was written – in his head anyway.

Matt Ryan saves it, it comes straight back out to Adam, the empty net beckons. Our hearts go from the exalted feeling of the Second Coming to sinking painfully quickly as the inevitable happens, the injustice of it all, a moment we will look back on as pivotal in our relegation from the Premier League.

Then out of nowhere comes our captain, centre half and local boy Lewis Dunk, 'He's one of our own, he's one of own, Lewis Dunk, he's one of our own,' to take out Adam as he went to pull the trigger. 'Take out' was the operative expression as Dunk took everything, apart from the ball itself, a challenge bordering on assault really. I waited for the ref to blow and award a second penalty, but it didn't happen.

Adam, I think, inadvertently helped us. In his embarrassment at missing after going to such lengths to take the kick, he just grabbed the ball and ran off with it to take the corner as quickly as possible like a scalded dog. I reckon the only explanation for all of this is that Adam was one of those kids growing up who owned the only decent football on the estate. So he therefore called all the shots about who played and the rules. He probably played up front as well, and had all the best players on his team. And when he had to go home for his tea, he took his ball with him so nobody else could play. Sorry, Charlie. Perhaps that was, in retrospect, a tad harsh.

Then in comes the first corner. Incredibly Charlie tries to score with it. Maybe my attempt at Janet and John psychology above was right after all – apology withdrawn, Mr Adam. He almost does score but Matt Ryan realises the danger in the nick of time and parries the ball away before it goes for a second corner.

Adam delivers again and this time it's headed by Mame Diouf like a bullet going straight for the roof of the net. But Albion winger Anthony Knockaert, probably the smallest man on the pitch, seems to develop Inspector Gadget-like qualities as he rises to head the ball off the line!

Wow, what a finish! Hearts racing and conversation flowing, myself and Jacob head back to the car. The length of the walk no longer matters. I will give our parking host a hug and a kiss, all is good with the world, and we have salvaged a point.

Then, taking me out of my reflections on the game with a jolt, I receive a text message. 'Where are you? You have parked in the wrong place and have blocked in my neighbours.'

What..?? I told my parking host that I was only 10 minutes away. The kisses were now dropped – a hug at best, my love. I went back to my parking instructions. Yep, 'Drive straight in and park in the space in front.' There had been two spaces in front: one housed the bins. I had been a bit unsure at the time.

I began to unpick what, at the time, seemed a perfectly straightforward decision. I was a cross between Poirot, Colombo & Bob Cryer from the Bill. It didn't make me feel any better.

Then we turned the corner into our street and I breathed a heavy sigh. As I looked forward, I could see the flats, the archway and two guys waiting there drinking cans of lager. Mmmm, this is going to get interesting. And to complicate things further, back to my role-model behaviour, it's just me and my 17-year-old son.

I went to walk past them, glancing first into the car park, which resulted in another sigh. There was a car positioned right in the middle blocking me in completely. I then heard the dulcet Staffordshire tones of one of the lager drinkers. 'Is that your fucking BMW mate? What do you think you're fucking doing? I've been blocked in all day, couldn't take my kids out.'

I turned to look at him and assessed the situation very quickly, a bit like Leonardo DiCaprio in *Inception*. This now felt like a parallel universe as well. My car was blocked in and this guy looked as if he wanted to punch me in the face, and fairly imminently at that. His mate was just staring at me intently. I had Jacob with me. I could go aggressive and take my chances in a fight, but even if I won that battle, my car was still stuck, so I couldn't leave, and who knows what other mates he has in the vicinity? This could escalate quickly.

Do you know what? On reflection, all that processing of thoughts in record time above comes from being a dad. If I had been with a mate, particularly certain mates I can think of – you know who you are – I'm sure I wouldn't have gone through that analysis of the situation and it would probably have ended badly.

But all of the above made my decision for me. Calling on that sales background, I was going in with charm and humour and not aggression, albeit ensuring that my eyes were telling him: 'I'm not going to be fucked about.' That's a difficult double act to pull off, you know.

The irony. Here I was again, having to explain the parking app and the system and that I had paid to park there. His mate was getting it, but the guy who wanted to hit me wasn't. What else did I have? Then miraculously I remembered her name. My parking host was Laura, this mythical figure who I had never met but was having such an impact on my life. The hug was off now as well, I thought, and she is getting one star at best on the review page on the app.

Her name magically brought my potential attacker out of his stupor and he responded to me: 'Laura lives in the flat upstairs. What has she got to do with it?' His mate was like Stephen Hawking in comparison to his friend and explained on my behalf. Phew – situation defused.

We concluded with a brief review of the game. Thank God it was a draw, so nothing to get too riled up about. Then he moved his car. His angry face had somehow lost its tension and we waved goodbye as friends; well, not really, but you know what I mean.

I never did meet Laura. I did wonder if she was looking down at us all that night in Stoke, thinking: 'All of this shit for a tenner!' I didn't have the heart to give her a poor review. Time to move on, Swansea at home next. No app required.

5. Self-harming

Why do we put ourselves through this − the pain, the angst, the nerves, the pressure, the financial cost and the time it all takes out of our lives?

It's not like going to the movies, a restaurant or the theatre. With all of these and most of our social commitments and interactions, we are pretty confident that we will have a great time, or at worst a pleasant day/evening.

You can read the reviews of the movie, you can watch the trailer, you can speak to friends who have seen it. You know if you like the actors, you know the type of films that hit the spot for you. The same for the theatre, the same for a restaurant. Then, of course, there are the people that you go with: your friends, relationships built up over years, many previous fantastic nights out to reflect on.

As we get older, we get fussier about the people we go out with. We don't have the time or energy for people who irritate us, bore us, dominate the conversation, are too serious, talk about work all the time, have no sense of humour, get old too soon in their outlook, are miserable, have a glass always half empty never half full et cetera, et cetera.

The venues we choose are researched in further detail: time is precious, after all. We have commitments, jobs, mortgages, kids, bills to pay and a never ending list of stuff to do. So when we finally get that spare spot in the diary, that chance to breathe, that evening to forget all of our responsibilities, we want it to be right, to be perfect, and to be a night to remember that we will reflect on in years to come.

So, the question has to be asked: 'Why the fuck do we go to watch football?'

It goes completely against everything I have just said. It's unpredictable: there is certainly no guarantee of entertainment. Quite the opposite, in fact; you can walk out of that ground devastated, emotionally drained, feeling physically sick. Yet you have paid for the pleasure.

It may also have taken you hours to get there; at least on the way there you are full of hope. After a heavy defeat that feeling of foreboding before you get in your car to drive or board a train for hours, painstakingly reviewing every minute detail of that horrific experience, that's when the self-harm starts.

You also start linking this event to all the other similar experiences you have had. It's a bit like a really bad hangover when you feel so ill and so low that you utter the immortal words: 'Right, that's it. I'm never drinking again.' It's the same with football: we self-analyse. Why am I doing it? What else could I be doing instead?

But in these times of adversity, what do we do? We sing our hearts out to remind ourselves that we like this and that we must come back. What's the alternative? A flat pack from IKEA to assemble, another room that needs a revamp at home? You know you are one step away from a Dulux colour chart at this point, or the dreaded supermarket run as you shuffle round like an inmate from *One Flew over the Cuckoo's Nest*, except that, in your case, escape is impossible.

But not only do we go through the self-loathing and questioning of our own sanity, we then pass this curse onto our loved ones, to our children: those same children that we will do anything for. We try to set them up for life with the right values, with purpose, to consider others, to be kind, to be driven and full of energy and passion for life. We would lay our lives on the line for them. Yet we saddle them with football, without a moment's hesitation, as some kind of life test.

We sell them the dream, the highs, the great goals, the trophies, the relegation escapes, the atmosphere, being very careful to conveniently miss out the other 90%, which is in essence the constant feeling of being let down, having promises not fulfilled and having moments of success ripped away from you at the last moment.

Yes, we happily pass that onto our children. 'Don't worry kids, it's like a drug and if you are truly addicted, it will never leave you for the rest of your life and you will be so hooked that you will pass it onto your children and so the circle of heartache and disappointment will continue from generation to generation.'

We try and justify this to ourselves and to our kids. After we lost 2-0 at West Brom, who hadn't won for 19 matches, I heard myself telling Jacob that this was character-building. He needed to experience these lows so that he could truly enjoy the highs that would inevitably follow.

You see? I missed out that this addiction will also cause you to lie to your children's faces – bare faced lying, just to make sure that they come back and take more of this drug with you. After all, it's no fun doing it on your own, is it?

I had to tell him again after we had done a ten-hour round trip and stood in the freezing cold watching wave after wave of Huddersfield attacks on our goal as our team of professional footballers seemed incapable of passing the ball to each other or – God forbid – getting close to that metal structure with netting and a bloke stood between two posts at the other end of the pitch.

Then at Everton we sat in wooden seats – not good for the older gentlemen: a sponsorship by Anusol would have been appropriate. The roof was so low that if the ball went over head height we couldn't see it. Multiple pillars were holding up this ancient stand, so you had to have the dexterity of a seasoned peeping tom to get any view of the game.

Which, as it turned out, was a blessing, as even getting the ball into Everton's half of the pitch seemed to take on a level of challenge comparable with negotiating peace in Northern Ireland, getting Arsène Wenger to admit he was wrong or convincing Simon Cowell that the waistband of his trousers didn't need to end up just below his nipples.

Finally, these medieval facilities extended to the gents' toilets, which were only suitable for a small child with no sense of smell. In summary, we travelled in the car for around 12 hours in one day and watched our worst performance of the season in complete discomfort.

So, we do self-harm, every gouge we make somehow making us crave more. Every cut – the shooting pain, the long term ache – making us still shake with expectation for the next fix. When we are not there in person, we still have the methadone that is Gary Lineker on *Match of the Day* to fill the gap so we can still function. As Sir Alex Ferguson said when interviewed live in 1999 after securing the Champions League to win a historic treble for Manchester United, 'Football, bloody Hell,' before retiring to the dressing room to watch a re run of the big match.

6. The Overnighter

Sometimes a day just isn't enough. You have to remind yourself of the fact that the prime reason for doing this is enjoyment. So trying to cram, say, 12 hours of driving plus a match into one day is not complementary to that objective, or safe for that matter. You are not a contestant on a Bear Grylls- style survival programme, after all.

This is where the case for an overnight trip becomes almost unanswerable, a necessity if you will. Just when you thought you had done all of your research and internal selling at home to make this project a reality, you realise you have to go again.

It's like the training they use in the Special Air Service [SAS], when they start the troops on a fitness challenge but don't tell them how long it will take, and just go on and on until they physically or mentally break. So I composed myself, took a deep breath and emphasised to my wife not the enhanced enjoyment that I would benefit from with an overnighter, but instead focused in on the safety aspect of this decision.

It's awful, isn't it? Using your son's potential demise (yes, I say 'son's' because I'm under no illusion that I'm not just collateral damage here!) and the associated guilt trip solely to justify the additional night away and, of course, those incremental costs incurred.

Well as the SAS motto says, 'Who Dares Wins' (also used with less gravitas by Del Boy in *Only Fools and Horses*). I made it, another step on the way to securing our mission achieved, with my marriage still intact. Now I needed to convince unsuspecting family members of their pivotal role in my plans.

The decision to travel there and back in a day to away games is clearly driven by the distance involved, but there are also many other points to consider if hotels are not in the budget secured with Mrs Clarke. The list is longer than you may think.

Does it fit in with your travel plans? Are minimal detours required to get there? Well, you have to be practical, you know.

Will your hosts be pleased to see you? This is key: are they looking forward to your visit, or is it one they felt that had to say yes to? Behind closed doors, are they are cursing you? Groaning about how inconsiderate you have been to even ask and how inconvenient it is? God, you may even want feeding – the cheek of it!

Are you able to get some sleep? (Trust me, at my age and with my back this is a consideration that I'm sad to say is gaining more and more priority with me) Will there be an actual bed? The sofa? The floor?

The first overnight experience was with Uncle Dan, now living at Leamington Spa, just south of Birmingham. Dan is now a university lecturer in Science at Warwick. I'm not sure what I'm more surprised about: that Dan is able to regularly stand up and talk/present to over 150 students every week without breaking into a cold sweat, suffering total paralysis through fear, or maybe being embarrassed by a slight incontinence issue and bemoaning the fact he selected chinos to wear that morning (he has always been very reserved, you see); or that we get on so well. They say opposites attract: we are definitely that, and football has always acted as a great bridge between us. Once across it, we are comfortable on any topic with each other.

So, travel plans – tick. It's Manchester United away at the end of November. I could do it in a day, having done the north-west many times that way. But then there is the weather and it would be good to see Uncle Dan. I needed a positive, as I was expecting to get whacked by José Mourinho's team, assembled with a net spend of circa £300m (poor José – it's still not enough, apparently). A few beers afterwards and Match of the Day would be the perfect pick-me-up.

Pleased to see us – tick. Dan wouldn't openly admit this of course. Along with enjoying our company, we would also be the first to visit his flat in Leamington Spa.

Getting some sleep – no tick here. Dan has one bedroom and one bed. It was sofa/inflatable-mattress-with-sleeping-bag time. I wasn't looking forward to this; I would need to be suitably inebriated before bedtime to get through it, and an early start was required to get Jacob back in time for his Worthing game. The two of them had conspired – whether or not intentionally is by the by – to make my overnight stay one of endurance.

Interrupted sleep, early morning wake up, a drive to Worthing, finished off with three and a half hours at the football, as the players need to be there 90 minutes before kick-off. I would need the mental strength of Terry Waite to get through this one. Okay, okay – slightly unfair: being kidnapped and held hostage for four years is not really comparable, and I did have a sleeping bag as opposed to being chained to a radiator. Terry also forgave his captors: something I am yet to do with Dan and Jacob.

Brighton played exceptionally well at Old Trafford, our best away performance of the season, but United are the experts at not playing well and getting a result. 1-0, and to make it worse Ashley Young was the goal scorer (I'm surprised he stayed on his feet long enough) and then – the depths of despair – a deflection as well.

'Typical United,' I muttered repeatedly in the car from Manchester to Uncle Dan's, to myself as much as Jacob. To stay on the political theme above (Terry W), the result was a travesty on the scale of George W Bush stealing the 2000 US election from Al Gore after the Florida re-count. Or, from a sporting perspective, Thierry Henry's handball that prevented the Republic of Ireland from reaching the World Cup Finals in 2010.

A few BrewDogs later and I had reported back to Uncle Dan. A few more and I basked in the positive feedback for Brighton on Match of the Day. A few more and I dozed off to sleep on sofa cushions on the floor.

Then I woke up in the middle of the night, desperately needing a wee and realising that I couldn't move. I got up slowly, each piece of my body getting itself into place. It was like Robert Downey Junior assembling as Iron Man.

I surveyed the wreckage around me, which was Jacob, and stepped over him into the bathroom. Through squinting eyes I saw that it was also now snowing. As I offloaded, I only had time to consider two things: I'm never sleeping on Dan's floor again; and I don't think a Grand National winner could piss as long as this. I pictured lights going on all around the neighbourhood, people woken up by my Niagara-like waterfall of urine. I then drifted off standing up, mumbling a Stone Roses tune that seemed to fit the moment.

Next was Newcastle away, staying at Charles and Madeline's. They live just outside Rotherham, which I have to admit I needed to look up (South Yorkshire, just north-east of Sheffield).

So, travel plans – tick. It's Newcastle away, our longest trip of the season at circa 350 miles, which on a good run with a couple of breaks would take around seven hours. There and back in a day? Not an option, unless I wanted to risk myself and Jacob waking up in a ditch, in intensive care somewhere, or not at all for that matter.

Add to the mix that it's December 30th, it hadn't escaped my attention that this was the riskiest fixture in terms of scuppering our plans for the 100% away record: bad weather, closed roads, you get the picture. So an extra early start was required, with a stop on the way back.

Charles is my father-in-law and Madeline is his fifth wife. That isn't a typo. Jo's Mum (Jenny) and Charles split up when Jo was very young, so Charles became more part of Jo's life from her university years onwards.

I've had many chats with Charles re his five wives, especially over numerous bottles of port at his place with Madeline in Portugal. In summary, Jenny was the first and the only one he had children with (Jo and Justin) and Madeline is the last and they have been together for 20-plus years. Wives two to four were the quick-fire round! To be fair, he always left them with the house and on reasonable terms, highlighted by a big birthday celebration for his mum with all five in attendance. Liz Taylor has nothing on Charles.

Madeline is a people-pleaser and will shower you with numerous compliments before you can take a breath, to the point where she renders you speechless as you literally have no response left to her super-sized acknowledgement of every aspect of your life, bless her. This is of course is also a tick for being made welcome.

On the sleep front – to be reviewed: no bed, but a double mattress brought downstairs that will also involve sleeping with Jacob.

Newcastle away was goalless and uneventful as a game. The most disappointing element was the Geordie fans, always lauded for the incredible atmosphere that they create and for their loyalty. Well, the noise levels were non-existent from the home end and I think their loyalty is over rated as well. I can recall them calling for the head of many a manager early and making his life and the feeling around the ground very uncomfortable.

However, in contrast, Chris Hughton, our manager, got a fantastic reception. He had been sacked as Newcastle manager in 2010, like many before him. Since Kevin Keegan (their Messiah) left in 1997 they have made 20 different appointments, some coming back multiple times. But this was an occasion when the fans didn't agree: Hughton had got them promoted to the Premier League and they were outside the relegation places when his career there was prematurely ended. He also goes down in history with the best win percentage of any Newcastle manager at just under 60%.

Outside of the Hughton reception, the only other high point (apart from the location of our seating, the game below resembling an ants' nest that had been aggressively disturbed) was seeing Sir John Hall outside the ground.

Sir John (85 now) is Life President and a former chairman of Newcastle. He took over in 1992 and replaced Osvaldo Ardiles as manager with Keegan. He saved them from relegation to the third tier and led them to the Premier League, where, in 1996, they famously ran Manchester United very close for the title.

They should have won it. They were 12 points clear at one point and unfortunately Keegan had a meltdown, instigated by the wily and experienced United manager, Alex Ferguson, and culminating in Keegan's 'I would love it if we beat them' rant live on Sky Sports after another defeat.

Sir John presided over Newcastle's best period of football in my lifetime. They were everyone's second-favourite team owing to the entertaining brand of football that they played, and the ethos was if you score four, we will get five. The only blot on Sir John's record, in hindsight, was selling out to Mike Ashley, who has become a very unpopular chairman (there go the Newcastle fans again). But in summary, Sir John was charming, approachable and it was lovely to have met him.

On the journey back, Jacob's cold, which had been evident that morning, was getting steadily worse. By the time we got to Charles and Madeline's he was barely able to get a sentence out without sneezing. They were insistent on taking us out for dinner, but Jacob now looked like shit and every time they asked him a question I was fearful that he would cover both them and their dinner in a shower of snot.

We got through unscathed and I had the pleasure of sleeping with Jacob as he grunted, moaned and sneezed through the night whilst having approximately half a toilet roll stuffed up each nostril. I can't entirely blame him for that as he learnt that tactic from me. What a legacy I have left him.

We left early after little sleep, thanked our hosts and Jacob kindly left them a gift of his cold, which Madeline reminded us of afterwards. Come on M, where are the compliments when we need them?

7. When It's All Worth It

West Ham away at the London Stadium, formerly the Olympic Stadium. This new venture had not run smoothly or without incident and controversy for the fans of the Hammers – also called the Irons, a name which dates back to when the club was formed in 1895 as Thames Ironworks F.C., effectively the works team for the last surviving shipbuilder on the River Thames.

The fans really did not want to leave their home in Upton Park, where they had been located since 1904, known as the Boleyn Ground because some believe that Anne Boleyn – Henry VIII's second wife – lived in Green Street House, located in what became the stadium car park.

We football fans are a sentimental bunch. You see, all our history has been played out in those grounds on the hallowed turf, even though we know it will have been replaced multiple times. But you can hear the echoes of songs sung and goals scored. It sparks the emotion in you and you can genuinely feel it when you walk into these places.

It's also the familiarity and even the routine. Lots of fans will drink in the same pub pre game, will take the same journey to the ground, and put a bet on at the same bookies. I had one mate who would have a haircut at the same barber shop!

That sentimentality is tied up with superstition as well, lucky pants being a favourite. You should see the state of some of them straining at the seams literally to cup the weight of the owners' testicles that aren't called into action often enough.

Then there were the circumstances in which West Ham acquired the new stadium. 'On the cheap' is an understatement. Spurs and Leyton Orient football clubs led the way in calling it out publicly in the press via their high-profile and charismatic chairmen, Daniel Levy and Barry Hearn. Their view was that West Ham got a stadium worth £600m for around £30m.

Levy requested government confirmation that West Ham would always have to keep an athletics track at the ground, concerned that they could become a top-three club in London on the back of what was effectively a state subsidy. Hearn was concerned that Orient could be wiped out altogether.

But West Ham Vice-chairman Karen Brady (now Baroness Brady), co-star of *The Apprentice* along with a certain Lord Sugar (just plain Alan when he was Spurs chairman - some interesting conversations must have been had there) navigated the deal through along with the West Ham co-chairmen; David Gold and David Sullivan.

Gold is an East End boy done good from Stepney and had interests in adult magazines, Ann Summers is still part of his business empire. As for Sullivan, born in Wales, but an Essex boy in Hornchurch from age 11, he owned the Daily & Sunday Sport newspapers as well as being involved in the adult magazine and sex industry, serving 71 days in prison at one point for living off immoral earnings.

Wealth is no guarantee of taste. Gold turns up to games looking like he could be an extra in *Goodfellas*. You could picture him stamping on the face of an opposing chairman, Joe Pesci-style, for a minor critique of the jellied eels. Sullivan has the attire of a Putin KGB enforcer. Journalists beware: a word out of place and a small but lethal injection could be administered by one of his minions as he sits in his boardroom stroking a white cat on his lap singing *I'm Forever Blowing Bubbles*.

Back to the game, a Friday night match. Fantastic – under the floodlights. Walking to the ground with Jacob was incredible, the skyscrapers of Canary Wharf overlooking the Olympic Stadium that shone like a beacon in the London night sky, picking out every detail of excitement, anticipation and hope on the faces of both sets of fans. Then in the distance "West Ham United" in claret letters glowing and beckoning you in. The expectation was building.

What is it about playing and watching under the lights? It's as if everything goes into High Definition: the grass is somehow greener, the images of the players and fans crisper and the noise is louder. It could also, of course, be alcohol-fuelled as supporters chuck down as many lagers as possible in that limited period between finishing work and kick off. Those beers are like a relentless Jürgen Klopp style *Gegenpress*; hunting the bar staff in packs and taking the beer rather than the ball from them, with the goal being to get it into the stomach at speed, more in the direct style of play of say a Sam Allardyce or a Tony Pulis than with the intricacies of a Klopp or Guardiola.

At West Ham, though, we have a paradox. We fans have experienced that inspirational walk from the station to the ground with that firework display of colours across the London sky. The beer and banter has us yearning for kick off time, then we are inside and the realisation hits. This isn't a football ground, it's an athletics stadium! Our seats are too far from the pitch and the atmosphere resembles a buffet with limp out-of-date sandwiches, cold tea and warm beer.

Now we know why the Hammers fans are so pissed off, robbed of their identity and history. At The Boleyn, the fans were so close to the pitch that you could tap a player on the shoulder before a throw in if you wanted to. I remember ex Hammers legend Julian Dicks playing for Liverpool at The Boleyn. The ball went into the crowd, and while he waited for it to be returned, a number of West Ham fans took the opportunity to shake his hand.

No danger of that at the Olympic Stadium. You would have needed a zip wire to get anywhere near the players and the pitch. Whereas The Boleyn rocked, treading the fine line between a great atmosphere and outright intimidation of the opposition, this place was more boy band ballad singer than Liam Gallagher — if you know what I mean (yeah, yeah – sorry!!).

From a Brighton perspective the game was amazing. It turned out to be our best away win of the season, 3-0. Glenn Murray scored after 10 minutes against the run of play and the killer goal from West Ham's perspective came just before half time as José Izquierdo, our new Colombian signing from Bruges, curled one into the top corner. Goalkeeper Joe Hart got a hand to it but it wasn't enough, although in his Manchester City title winning prime he might have saved it. The whistle blew, the West Ham players' confidence was now dented beyond repair, and, more importantly, the heat from the home fans had been significantly turned up. They had started unhappy and as the players walked off the pitch, there was a crescendo of boos and personal abuse.

The third goal went in from the penalty spot, again scored by Murray, a 34 year old journeyman pro, who had been with us before at the Withdean when we went up into the Championship in 2011 as Champions of League One. A fallout followed with then manager Gus Poyet and before we knew what happened he was scoring 30 goals for our arch-rivals Crystal Palace.

He was now a returning hero, part of the team who went up to the Premier League and there were whispers in the press about an England call up – incredible. He was my favourite player at the Withdean, so even when he was at Palace I refused to join in with the boos. He gained additional respect by not celebrating any of his goals against Brighton.

It was great to have him back and he had now made our Friday night in the smoke! We were in a state of euphoria on so many levels; an away win, we had scored three goals, we had a clean sheet and we were under the lights. ALBION, ALBION the crowd roared: we had an atmosphere in here after all.

Then I looked round at the rest of the stadium and it was a mass exodus of West Ham fans. Now you always get the odd individuals who seem to delight in leaving early so they can shave potentially 20 minutes off their journey home. Sod the fact that the most exciting and pivotal moments in many matches happen in the dying moments. Why do those people go?

This was different. Two-thirds of the stadium had left in record time. I thought: 'The Wembley stadium management need to pay a visit here. The West Hams fans have perfected what they have failed to achieve for the last 30 odd years – a speedy exit from a stadium.'

We were left to sing alone, our voices echoing around this empty shell – 'Three-nil to the Albion', 'Can we play you every week?' et cetera, et cetera.

8. Lennon & McCartney it ain't...

Singing at football matches has been a tradition for as long as I can remember and of course this is one of the great benefits of going 'Away'.

What has happened to home crowds? Even at grounds renowned for atmosphere such as Anfield and Stamford Bridge, if you go when the match is not against one of the top six or a Champions League game then it can be incredibly quiet. The locals often blame it on the 'Football Tourists' from overseas or the ever increasing corporate areas, containing spectators christened 'The Prawn Sandwich Brigade' by Roy Keane at Manchester United.

It is hard to say as a Brighton fan, but one of the best atmospheres in the Premier League now is actually generated by the 'Ultras' at Crystal Palace. Selhurst Park is rocking, in particular at mid-week night games.

At the Amex, some of the loudest crowds have been inspired by a sense of injustice. I remember one game I took my Dad to when Gus Poyet was manager. It was against Burnley and we were down to nine men in the first 20 minutes. The crowd as well as Gus were going crazy and it lasted the whole game for both of us. I thought Gus's head was going to explode like the guy in the 80s David Cronenberg science fiction horror film *Scanners* (we lost 1-0).

But go away from home and you are guaranteed that atmosphere throughout the 90 minutes pretty much, whilst standing the whole time. Why can't we sing sitting down? (A government study and think tank is required here, methinks).

But all that said, where singing is concerned, it's still about the quality of the lyrics for me. My favourite bands are the Arctic Monkeys and Oasis and as much as I love the music, what sets them apart is the writing of Alex Turner and Noel Gallagher respectively, modern day poets.

As a result I want the same from my football songs. They should be clever, funny and often the simpler the better. The first I remember hearing (not at a game but on the TV), which got repeated in school playgrounds everywhere was 'Georgie Best, Superstar, he walks like a woman and he wears a bra!' Now it's clearly of its time (the 60s) and would be viewed now as super sexist (Megan wouldn't approve). But do you know what? It was simple and funny.

Another classic of that ilk was about Sammy Lee, the very small and rotund Liverpool midfielder: 'He's fat, he's round, he bounces on the ground, Sammy Lee, Sammy Lee'

Also of that genre 6 foot 7 inch striker Peter Crouch, when at Liverpool 'He's big, he's red, his feet stick out the bed – Peter Crouch, Peter Crouch'.

At Arsenal: 'Vieira, whoa-oh, Vieira whoa-oh-oh-oh; he comes from Senegal, he plays for Arsenal!' Repeat several times – you get the gist.

Then there are the ones that go into a bit more detail, not purely observations but with some back-story as well. For example Fernando Torres at Liverpool:-

'His armband proved he was a red Torres Torres
You'll Never Walk Alone it said Torres Torres
We bought the lad from sunny Spain
He gets the ball and scores again
Fernando Torres, Liverpool's number nine.'

'Na na na na na na na na, Na Na, Na Na,
na na na na na na na na, Na Na, Na Na,
na na na na na na na na na na na na na na na

FERNANDO TORRES Liverpool's No.9!'

(Truly inspired at the end - Turner, Gallagher, Lennon, and McCartney – their vocabulary just never reached these heights of literary prose).

And at Brighton for South American striker Leonardo Ulloa who replaced previous terrace hero Glenn Murray, who left for arch rivals Crystal Palace:-

'Who's that man from Argentina?
Who's that man we all adore?
Leanardo is his name
and he scored a goal again
and we don't miss Murray anymore.'

So these songs are not particularly inspired, but they work at football grounds, you see. Look at the most famous of all, *Football's Coming Home* – great lyrics on the record, but the beauty was the simplicity in the stadiums: 'It's coming home, it's coming home, it's coming, football's coming home.'

My pet hate is the repeated songs. They are like the box set. One set of fans invents and everyone else follows, just replacing the player's name, with no imagination or flair. Come on guys, we need more than that. Essentially the Stock, Aitken and Waterman of football chants, examples below:-

'He's one of our own, he's one of our own - INSERT LOCAL PLAYER'S NAME – he's one of our own.'

'We've got – INSERT PLAYER'S SURNAME – INSERT PLAYER'S FIRST NAME AND SURNAME – you just don't seem to understand. He only cost a mill, he's better than Ozil, we've got – INSERT PLAYER'S FIRST NAME & SURNAME.'

I can also sometimes refuse to sing a song if it sticks in the throat because of its complete factual inaccuracy, a classic being one about Brighton midfielder Dale Stephens, to the tune of Earth, Wind & Fire's *September*:-

'Ayee Ay, Stephens our midfielder' (ok so far)

'Ayee Ay, he plays with Davy Propper' (factually true, yes)

'Ayee Ay, he never gives the ball away.' (Come on!!)

On the away trips there were a few people who inserted the word 'seldom' in place of 'never' which I did like. See? A subtle change and a sense of irony can make all the difference.

You do get the odd throwback song to yester year, mostly highly inappropriate, but sometimes they just re appear as a one-off, never to be heard again.

David Beckham got awful stick all around the country at every away ground after being sent off for England against Argentina at the World Cup. It went too far, songs about his wife, Victoria (perhaps better-known then as Posh Spice), and burning effigies of him at West Ham. Ironically it seemed to inspire him; he had his best season ever and turned most people's frustration into grudging respect.

Weirdly, some wannabe 18 year old Brighton Ultras attempted to resuscitate this genre with some lyrics involving 'Posh' and Lewis Dunk (Brighton's 'one of our own' centre half), which don't warrant being repeated here and also would give this book a X rating (how old am I?– sorry for you younger readers - an 18 that is!)

However, I can't resist sharing the following homage to 70's and 80's football hooliganism, my mate Sid told me he heard this one at a non-league game in Middlesex:

'Hayes & Yeading, we'll kick your f****n' head in.' Is it wrong to admit that that one made me laugh?

It's the classics, though, that will live on: *You'll Never Walk Alone*, *Blue is the Colour*, *When the Saints Go Marching In* and at Brighton the less well-known *Sussex by the Sea*, handed down from generation to generation. These are the Lennon & McCartneys, never going out of fashion.

Why not try and write one yourself? I dare you...

9. Homeboy

I realise that I have made going to watch an away match the nirvana of the football experience, but of course it may not be for everyone. After all we have around 30,000 every week at the Amex for the home games, but only around ten percent of those go away, typically anything between 1,500 and 3,000. Yes, there are ticket restrictions and allocations that come into play, but I wouldn't expect to see 25,000 going on their travels every week even if those didn't exist.

So, let me introduce you to Finlay, my younger son who doesn't subscribe to the away nirvana theory, but is there more often than not at the Amex and has done some of the harder yards pre Premier League. Not the full heartache of Brighton's football experiences, I grant you, but he can't help the fact that he was born in 2004.

However, this is a key marker for the Clarke family in footballing terms as Fin is the only member of our clan born in the catchment area of Brighton, in Worthing to be precise. In fact my wife Jo was pregnant with Fin when we made the move from south-west London to West Sussex. This re-location of course established the Brighton connection for us all in the first place.

Fin was a late starter in football terms. Always different, always creative. It started with his clothes: he would regularly cut sleeves off hoodies, wear odd socks and could produce some very inspired outfits. He even turned up to his introductory day at his new middle school wearing an 'Artful Dodger'-style top hat, which clearly made an impression on the headmaster who greeted him by name on his first day at the school: 'Morning Finlay, no hat today then?'

His first club was not a football one. It was Stagecoach, where he could funnel his quirky style with like-minded people. His teacher said he was very creative but mad as a box of frogs!

In later years he would do numerous auditions for the main part of Woody in *Toy Story*. Not that unusual, you might think. However, the first we heard of it as parents was when the school phoned us at home to make sure we were okay with the big commitment to rehearsals as he had the lead role. 'Typical Fin,' we said together.

Fin also has a fascination with all things Japan, including the Anime films, and has always liked K-Pop – that's Korean Pop to the uninitiated. So the more traditional young lad route into football had to find its way into Fin's busy schedule of commitments.

To be honest, I never expected it to happen and I was equally enjoying Fin's exploits and explorations of a number of areas that were new to me also. Then, out of the blue: 'Dad, I want to join a football team – I've got some mates at Worthing Dynamos.' And our football story together was born.

Fin started to alternate trips to the Amex with Megan and Jacob. He was the polar opposite of Jacob from the moment he got in the car to when we arrived and walked into the ground. It was non-stop talking about Brighton, his favourite players, school, mates, Japan, K-Pop, family, the dog, politics, the news and a hundred 'Why' questions. Sounds intense, but I loved it (and still do).

No middle class footy for Fin; all he wanted was a pie (sometimes two – pre game and at half time!) and to get into his seat as soon as possible. There were two types of Fin at the footy: either he was totally disengaged and 'tired,' or he was full-on to the extreme, with some very extravagant goal celebrations.

At heart Fin is a 'Homeboy,' and stuck almost exclusively to the Amex. He did do a couple of Fulham away trips as we have friends there, the most memorable being when Tomer Hemed scored an injury time penalty winner at the away end, which was packed to the rafters. We all went crazy; Fin had stood on his seat for the entire game between myself and Jacob and I can still picture the joy on his face as we all hugged together with him sandwiched in the middle.

The only concern with Fin was that he had become my conscience where money was concerned in the season where myself and Jacob were going for our 100 percent set of away games. He had obviously been listening in the background to some of the inevitably vociferous chats between myself and Jo when a chunk of cash needed to be spent on the house.

I shudder at the memory of when the argument was at its peak and Jo would take me to the point of no return by muttering: 'Well, how much have you and Jacob spent on those away trips so far?' Occasionally, like a vet administering that final lethal injection to put me out of my misery, she backed it up with: 'I know it's not *just* the tickets. What about petrol, food and overnight stays?'

My head now spinning as I took a virtual standing eight count, I could feel the ref's arms around my shoulders as he told me that I'd taken enough punishment for one day. Unfortunately there would be re-matches (more like mis-matches) throughout the season, with the same inevitable result. Still, it was part of the pain that I would need to man up to, so that Jacob and I could complete our righteous journey to that last away game at Anfield. The punishment endured would mean an even sweeter savouring of that final goal being achieved. That's what I kept telling myself anyway.

However, what I hadn't counted on was that Finlay, quietly observing on a stealthy mission that the SAS would have been proud of, was not only listening but clearly taking notes of the key data points from our discussions. Knowing Fin, he probably did some follow-up analysis of which points made the most impact: he was like a general of psychological warfare, waiting for his moment to pounce on his unsuspecting father.

Fin would select his time carefully: perhaps during an argument that he was clearly losing, or a discussion around a new purchase for Fin (he doesn't ask for much, but when he does he goes big – for example, 'Dad, I really need a gaming computer.' 'Oh yeah? How much are those, Fin?' 'A bottom of the range one is about three grand!!'). Sometimes, butting into a heated discussion/ argument between myself and Jo, leveraging the 'good cop' routine with mum so as to cash in later when the time is right! Maybe to reduce Jacob's chances of getting what he wants when he is trying to squeeze some more cash out of his parents. Or to instigate a pincer movement with Megan, whom he gets onside as a fellow- sufferer of this perceived family injustice.

The optimum moment selected, Fin then starts launching the bombs in. Some, full frontal attacks in the heat of the battle: 'Well, maybe we could afford it if you didn't spend so much money going to the football, Dad.' Others casually tossed in from behind the screen of his laptop as he sits on the sofa, appearing to be paying no attention to what is going on: 'How much does it cost to fill up our car, Dad?' And finally, the exit bomb that he detonates as he leaves the room, to simmer before exploding with catastrophic effect, normally in my face: 'Dad, how much is that hotel costing?'

Over time, of course, I got wise to these attacks and had counter-strategies ready and prepared to put into action (being the 'adult' in this relationship). Even with pre-prepared plans though, the Fin-and-Megan pincer movement was in another league. Enter this one and it could be a bloody war with a huge amount of collateral damage and casualties left on the battle field. Sometimes it was wiser to stay out of it and take some of the negative press on the chin!

Fin is unique and I love him for it. He was also the earliest fan of Lewis Dunk that I know of, especially for his age – unusual to have a centre half as a kid's favourite. Lewis 'he's one of our own' Dunk went on to be one of the players of the season for Brighton as well as captain when Bruno was absent.

So the 'Homeboy' can add talent-spotter to psychological general and, of course, pie connoisseur to his footballing credentials. Preferring home to away matches pales into insignificance against these achievements.

10.   Loneliness & the Long-distance Radio Phone-In

Now I have spoken about Jacob and his long bouts of unconsciousness on our car journeys. So the question is: when you don't have a 'guest' on the trip, what do you do whilst you're waiting for your son to come out of hibernation?

The iPod is, of course, a saviour and I can get fired up to the Arctic Monkeys & Oasis, get aggressive with Stormzy, Wiley & Plan B, go for some pop with Justin Timberlake or go old school with Elvis, The Everly Brothers or Simon & Garfunkel. I will leave it to you to decide which ones were influenced by the kids and which are my own.

But I always end up turning to the radio and in particular my addiction to talkSPORT and, to a lesser extent, BBC Radio 5 live. On the journey to the game I'm full of hope, so it's more about the build-up to the big games which raise your expectations and excitement.

However, on the way back you have had the outcome. You are either ecstatic, cruising down the motorway re-running those wonderful goals you have scored in your mind with a soppy grin on your face. Or conversely you are bitter, twisted and needing to vent on someone or something. At this point, listening to the radio is no longer enough. I now need to participate.

It has to be said, as well, that my need to get involved can also be sparked by the absolute bullshit being spouted by the presenters or people dialling in. It's their job to draw me in, I know, and sometimes I just can't help myself.

Brighton's over-achievement under Chris Hughton, the lack of recognition on *Match of the Day* and the fake news around transfer spending have all got me on, talking to footballing 'legends' like Robbie Savage or Joey Barton.

It's sort of therapeutic as well to hear other fans that are going through your pain. It's as if we are all wandering the corridors of an asylum ranting, moaning, laughing and crying, and just can't find our way out. The phone-in gives us that glint of light and the hope that we can and will get through this.

As supporters, there is also a hint of jealousy as well – how have these guys managed to get a well-paid job talking about football, when we do it for free multiple hours in a day? I know it's harder than it looks, but if Paul Scholes can do it after barely speaking to the media for 15 years, then we all have half a chance, don't we?

In fact that thought must have been lodged in the dark recesses of my mind as, while at home one evening in 2015, I was listening to talkSPORT and heard them announce that they were launching a five-month campaign to find the UK's most talented fan to become the 'People's Pundit.' The prize was to broadcast live from a Premier League game on the last day of the season. Jeff Stelling of Sky Sports was fronting the competition.

This took me back to childhood memories of commentating and taping mock sporting interviews with my mate Bill in the privacy of my bedroom at home. We did boxing, cricket and football mainly: the excitement we generated in each other was intoxicating. I still remember vividly the uncontrollable laughter, as I should point out these were all piss-takes of the real thing, not serious attempts at journalism. A forerunner to Alan Partridge; we were just ahead of our time!

As we got older, and with the introduction of alcohol into our lives , a metamorphosis occurred into something very random, that I'm not sure I've shared with anyone before. Well, here goes.

We started going round to Bill's a lot as he always had a free house. His Dad was usually down at the pub and his mum had sadly passed away when he was very young. We didn't look old enough to get served at the local pub, but somehow had just enough bum fluff on our youthful faces to get beers from the off license. So, indoor drinking at Bill's became our sport: me, Bill, his brother Geoff and another mate, Mark.

I'm not sure quite how this started, but one night after many lagers we decided (I'm not sure whose idea it was; it must have been spawned by our spoof radio interviews, so I'm going for collective responsibility here!) that I would ring up random semi strangers (typically talking to parents of kids we knew, but not too well) pretending to be a radio DJ running a phone in, advising the unsuspecting recipients of my call that they had been nominated by a friend or family member to take part in a quiz, and informing them that they were live on air and that there were prizes to be won.

One particular night we were talking to the dad of a partial mate who only lived a few doors down. He was so excited (I'm ashamed to admit), not just because he was on live radio, but because his son, who barely ever spoke to him, had nominated him. Oh God, when I look back now.

But the reaction in the room at my end was incredible. Bear in mind that we are talking phones in the old days here, with no loud speakers. So all my mates could hear was my end of the conversation and they had to be silent so as not to give the game away. My first audience! (Unless you count playing a comedian called Pablo in the middle school Christmas production of *Zorro* – no I don't quite get that 'festive' choice either.)

I can see their faces now. They were doubled up on the sofa, bright red, eyes glazed from cans of Tennent's with pictures of girls on! Remember them? Wow, they seem like prehistoric times now, don't they? And holding in the laughter so much that they resembled Violet Beauregarde in *Charlie and the Chocolate Factory,* as she began to expand into a giant blueberry about to explode before the Oompa-Loompas rolled her away. Great nights, but I must apologise to our victims. Sorry, guests.

Back to the People's Pundit. To enter the competition you needed to post a one-minute commentary on YouTube. I was so hooked on the concept that I literally did it that same night, badgering my daughter Megan to help me load it up.

What is the age when we become incapable of operating 'new' technology? My reaction to YouTube was the same as my dad's to operating the video recorder years before. Setting a timed recording could lead to a total meltdown for him before he handed over responsibility to me after pressing lots of buttons really hard.

Megan delivered and I was in.

Although in haste I had used a pink karaoke mic (one of Megan's old toys), I thought nothing of it at the time. But once I shared my clip with mates there were various comments along the lines of 'Yeah, you did a really good job mate, but why were you using a dildo for a mic?'

I made it to the next round; the use of a sex toy hadn't scuppered my chances after all. There were regional heats around the country and I was selected for Bristol - I think London was full. Luckily I had a team from work based there and they gave me some incredible vocal support on the night, which was even commented on by Ian Danter, who hosted from talkSPORT, referring to me as a 'home' candidate.

I commentated on Tony Yeboah's goal for Leeds United against Liverpool in front of the live audience, 'like an exocet missile' and the crowd roared in support, bless 'em. Then I had to pick a topic out of the hat to talk on for two minutes – Should Gareth Bale leave Real Madrid? The cut-down version of my verdict was 'No.' The panel, which included Bobby Gould, the former-Wimbledon and Wales manager, conferred for what seemed like an age before I was announced as the winner.

I was now part of the 'Final Five' and we attended boot camp at Wembley Stadium with Ray Parlour and the talkSPORT team. Each contestant was then attached to a talkSPORT show for the next three weeks, getting a task every Monday and reporting back every Friday live on air. I was linked to *Drive* with Adrian Durham and Darren Gough.

Task 1: I had to defend Brendan Rodgers' Liverpool live on air under a strong cross examination from Adrian and scouser and ex-footballer Micky Quinn. The feedback was that I had given as good as I got, especially with Adrian!

Task 2: The production of my own edited two-minute football story, *Footballers Past, Present & Future*. It focused on an ex Millwall pro, Damien Webber, whose career had been cut short by injury (a local fellow footy Dad in Worthing), moving onto Tommy Elphick, captain of Bournemouth, who were about to be promoted to the Premier League, and then finally the future with Bournemouth apprentice Baily Cargill, who is now at Milton Keynes Dons. Adrian had gone from attacking me in week one to letting me bask in the glory of his compliments in week two!

Task 3: the final task, the challenge of sourcing my own interview for broadcast on air, which would be rated on the level of the guest secured and how newsworthy the story was. I managed to secure two, interviewing both Brighton manager Chris Hughton and former

Uruguay, Chelsea and Spurs midfield player Gus Poyet. I went with Gus, as I managed to get him talking in detail about fellow countryman Luis Suarez's biting incidents, which was also very topical. To be fair I did get Chris Hughton reviewing the famous Hoddle and Waddle duet, *Diamond Lights,* but Gus just edged it.

Then the 'Final Five' were all invited to a bizarre lunch with partners in London, where an elongated session of small talk preceded the announcement that we were all waiting for. Jeff Stelling stood up and confirmed me as the *People's Pundit* winner in May 2015, the culmination of a five-month competition. Jo cried - tears of relief that it was all over, I think, and the hope that family life could return to normal.

My prize was magnificent: to broadcast live on air for talkSPORT at Liverpool legend Steven Gerrard's last game for the club. Incredibly Stoke smashed Liverpool 5-1. The good news was that I got plenty of air time as goal after goal went in. At least Stevie got a consolation one at the end and received a well-deserved standing ovation from all.

I then got to interview Peter Crouch after the game, as he had broken Alan Shearer's Premier League record for headed goals. This was a disturbing experience for me as at 6' 6", I'm not used to looking up at people. He was great, friendly from the off, unlike Mark Hughes, the Stoke manager. Even though his team had just won 5-1, he looked as if the interview process was the equivalent of a vasectomy being performed without anaesthetic by Abu Hamza the Egyptian Cleric (yes, the one with the hook hand. Come on, stay with me).

There were even a couple of spin-offs: a bit like doing *Knots Landing* after *Dallas*. They were a lot of fun, and I was very lucky, but I felt that I was milking my limited talent. Feel free to have a look on YouTube; I even had a proper mic by this stage.

They included interviewing Ray Lewington, the England assistant coach under Roy Hodgson, and appearing on the *Fletch & Sav* show, presented by commentator Darren Fletcher and former Wales midfielder Robbie Savage, where I interviewed former Liverpool and England goalkeeper David James outside Anfield before their FA Cup tie against West Ham. And finally - my favourite - getting to write in the Brighton programme every couple of home games on football topics of my choice under the People's Pundit heading.

During the process of the competition I always remember the first time we were invited into the talkSPORT studios. I was reminded of that thought/touch of jealousy around having a job to talk footy all day. The first guys I saw broadcasting live were Paul Hawksbee and Andy Jacobs. There was an ad break on at the time and one was reading the paper and the other was doing his emails on what looked like a BlackBerry (they still exist). I thought: 'This is either incredibly easy, or they are the consummate professionals with years of experience who can make it look that way.' I'm still not sure which one it is.

After winning the competition myself and Jeff Stelling were the guests of Sam Matterface and Stuart Pearce. I observed Pearcey and he couldn't have looked more uninterested as he thumbed through his tabloid of choice. Where was 'Psycho'? Where was the man who gave me one of my best ever live football experiences when he smashed that penalty in against Spain at Wembley during Euro 96? I realised at that moment what the expression 'hairs standing up on the back of your neck' meant and they have done so again every time I have watched it since!

Looking at Stuart now, talkSPORT appeared to be a sort of all-inclusive holiday resort for ex-professionals where he could eat and drink what he wanted, talk to the occasional stranger and get paid in between managerial/coaching roles and adverts. Good luck to him – and I certainly wouldn't tell him to his face.

So, back to the car (that was a record digression even by my standards so far). If Jacob does happen to wake up either during one of my phone in moments or while I'm waiting to go on, his face just screws up. 'Oh you're not doing it again, are you? What's the matter with you?' I am left in no doubt that I truly am both middle-aged and an embarrassing dad.

I can just about resist the urge to retort with: 'I'm sorry Jacob; after all, the last couple of hours with you has been littered with witty remarks, humorous stories and intelligent observations. In fact, if I closed my eyes it's almost as if I had raconteurs Peter Ustinov and David Niven right here with me in the car, when actually it was you all along – dickhead!'

talkSport People's Pundit Campaign

Tommy Elphick Bournemouth Captain & Ex Brighton

Chris Hughton, Brighton & Hove Albion Manager

Gus Poyet

talkSport People's Pundit Winner

Jeff Stelling Sky Sports

talkSport studio 'live on air' with Jeff Stelling

Kevin Clarke Commentating at Stoke v Liverpool

(Steven Gerrard's last game)

Peter Crouch

Ray Lewington

Harry Redknapp & Jacob

Jacob & 'Jamo'

Interview for BT Sport with David James

Jacob & Steve McManaman

Jacob 'Owen' Clarke & Michael Owen

The Peoples Pundit Brighton Programmes

The Peoples Pundit Articles

The Peoples Pundit Podcast with Ian Hart

George Dowell Chairman Worthing F.C.

11.　My Confession

Did you wonder why AWAY was half red and half blue on the title page? Maybe it hadn't crossed your mind? Well, here is the big reveal for those who either didn't work it out or don't give a monkey's!

I support two football teams. There I said it. It seems straightforward, doesn't it, when you write it down like that, matter-of-fact style? A non-football supporter, in particular backed by the information and logic to follow, I think would be very comfortable and would not see any problem with this.

But to a true football fan (I was going to say I count myself as one of those, but actually I know I'm one of those), this is a major issue.

When you start supporting, *truly* supporting a football team, there are some key, basic rules that come into play:

(i)　　Ideally, it should be your local team, where you were brought up.

(ii)　　Failing the above, support for that team should at least have been passed onto you by a member of your family, preferably father to son: old-fashioned, I know, so let's allow mother to daughter as well, or any family combination you want to come up with.

(iii)　　If not hitting either of the two above, you at least need to show loyalty. You have one team and you stick by them through thick and thin, regardless of results et cetera.

(iv)   In the best case, you are a season ticket holder; middle ground, you go occasionally; and in the worst case, you watch your team on the TV. If you can't even be bothered to do that, then you may as well withdraw from being a supporter anyway. Or maybe you are just faking it so you can join in pub conversations with your mates, which is even worse!

If you don't do, or are not interested in, any of the above, fine – you are not a football fan. However, it does mean that you will be treated with suspicion by true football fans, who think there must be something wrong with you.

My mate Reg (a Millwall fan, his support passed onto him by his dad who was a docker, so he has credibility on point's ii, iii and iv above) summed it up perfectly: 'Never trust a bloke who doesn't have Sky Sports.' My mate Rob responded: 'But *you* haven't even got Sky Sports, Reg.' To which Reg retorted: 'I know – but I've got Box Nation!' Argument settled. Look, I never said there was any logic to it!

Here is my story and why I only can tick rule (iv) above, even though I have been a total football addict for 45 years or so. The paradox is that the personal choices I have made create more angst, argument and debate with close friends (and, in particular, fellow football addicts) than Donald Trump, Nigel Farage, Brexit, immigration, gay marriage, taxation, women's rights, the environment and the #MeToo campaign all rolled into one.

So here we go. It starts at Stamford Bridge, the home of Chelsea FC. My grandad, Peter, and my Nana, Jenny, lived off the North End Road in Fulham, within walking distance of the ground. Fulham Broadway is the nearest station to Chelsea's stadium, whereas

Fulham's ground is actually closest to Putney Bridge (for the non-Londoners).

I always remember as a kid that my grandparents were the only people I knew who had a telephone, which gave them a sort of mythical status. So, if ever it rang I would be there in an instant to answer it, no matter where I was in the house at the time. On one occasion, I arrived at the phone after running on the R of ring.

'Hello, is Fred there please?'

I responded: 'No, sorry; you must have the wrong number. There is nobody called Fred here.'

'Are you sure? This is 01-356 2007, isn't it?' (I must warn you that I used to work for London Directory Enquiries and still have a weird, Derren Brown-like ability to remember random phone numbers. I can do Harrods, Selfridges, British Rail – oh, I'm so much fun at parties. Go on Kev, do that Buckingham Palace one again, it's brilliant!)

'Yes, that is the number, but no Fred here, I'm afraid. Goodbye.'

I rushed back into the small back room that we were all crammed into, me, Mum, Dad, my sister Tracy, Nana and Grandad. It was odd that they lived in a decent-sized house, but everyone lived in this room with a small kitchen off the back of it, where Grandad would wash and shave in the sink. They had a big front room, but that was 'for best', when guests came. It was immaculate, which was down to being rarely used. They also had a bathroom upstairs, but only for baths – why go all the way up there when you had a perfectly good sink in the kitchen?

I carried on with whatever I was doing in the back room, normally playing with cars, watching *Football Focus* or Laurel & Hardy with Grandad, or gaining endless amusement from hitting his artificial leg as hard as I could with a spoon, where he miraculously (to me) showed no sign of discomfort. He instigated this game, but it backfired on him dramatically when I belted the wrong leg on my first attempt one morning. I can still see the tears in his eyes.

Grandad was a bit of a worrier, and, coupled with the fact that phone calls were rarer than white dog shit (which ceased to exist at all from the early 80s) he asked: 'Who was it on the phone, Kevin?'

'Don't worry Grandad, it was a wrong number.'

'Who did they ask for?'

'They asked for Fred. I told them there was no Fred living here.'

'That's me' he proclaimed. 'Pam, Pam! He's put the phone down on someone trying to call me'.

So I then discovered that my Grandad, who everyone that I ever knew called Peter (including my Dad), had actually been christened Frederick Ernest, and some people – bizarrely, I know – actually called him by his real first name, Fred. Just for the record, I never found anyone subsequently who called him Ernie. But I wouldn't have been surprised, as I also then discovered that my Nana wasn't Jenny; she was actually a Jane but hated the name so much that she refused to answer to it. What is it with that generation? As a Kevin I'm starting to think I have missed a trick here.

Back to North End Road, which was also the family home where my mum, Pamela, and her sister Muriel (who we all called Lulu – I'm not even going there) had been brought up. As mentioned with reference to the spoon game, Grandad had an artificial leg. He enlisted in December 1942, during World War II, and took part in the largest seaborne invasion in history on D Day (June 6, 1944). The objective was the liberation of German-occupied France from Nazi control.

He and his colleagues from the Royal Artillery Gunners, along with many other soldiers, had been dropped from their boats on the French coast into water that was too deep with back packs that were too heavy. The inevitable result was that many didn't make it to the beach and dry land.

Grandad was one of the lucky ones in that, after being dragged under the boat and having his leg mashed up by the propeller, he was carried out of the water alive to relative safety on another ship. The first he knew was waking up in the army hospital, his leg needing to be amputated above the knee to save him from infection.

He was discharged just under a year later in May 1945. The war ended on August 15 with the surrender of Japan. Maybe not making it onto the beach saved his life. We will never know and he never spoke about it, like so many others. I think the memories were just too acute and painful.

This, though, didn't stop him walking to Stamford Bridge, where he had his season ticket as a lifelong fan – he ticked all my rules! I can still see him swinging that artificial leg that he would never get changed for a new light-weight one. He had a leather harness to keep it on; every stride was like Danny Frame tossing the caber. Look him up – I had to.

My mum and dad's first home was also in Fulham. Their first child, and my only sibling, Tracy, was born in St Stephen's Hospital, Chelsea.

My dad, Tony, came from a small village outside Canterbury and was more of a cricket fan. World War II to him was exciting. They were out of danger in the country and he was a kid watching a firework display in the sky every night while his village was transformed by the arrival of many American soldiers who had a camp nearby. He wasn't half as excited as the local women, by the way, according to some of his stories – but that's another book!

Village cricket was the main sporting activity, ahead of football, and of course Canterbury was the home ground of Kent County Cricket Club, which famously had a lime tree inside the boundary rope in the St Lawrence ground. If the ball hit it; however high up, it was still four runs.

I was told that so many times as a kid, and that simple fact filled me with such wonder that I had to get it in. I liked its unique quality: nobody else had a tree on their pitch. Imagine Brighton having a small apple tree in the corner of their goal. 'I don't care if the ball has beaten the keeper, if it hits that tree, the rules say no goal.' I'm going to suggest it to Mr Hughton. Staying up is based on fine margins, after all.

Dad had indoctrinated me into the sport, taking me to see Kent from when I was very young, which I loved. They had a great team in the 70's including legends like Alan Knott, Derek Underwood and Bob Woolmer. This carried on throughout Dad's life, but I haven't been to or watched a cricket match since he passed away.

On reflection I think there are two reasons: football was always my first love, and, in retrospect, all my enjoyment of cricket was about being there with him. We had some truly wonderful times, culminating in finally seeing Kent win something together. We went to five or six one-day finals at Lord's over the years and Kent lost every one. They were great days out, but a trophy would have been nice at some point, although it never stopped us going to the next one.

Then it happened. Kent made Finals Day of the Twenty20 Cup in 2007. It was to be held at Edgbaston, home of Warwickshire. Four teams, two semi-finals and a final, all played in a single day. It started at 10.30am, running through to 10pm, with alcohol being served all day to four sets of fans (in this case those of Kent, Lancashire, Gloucestershire & Sussex). Can you imagine that with football, say, Chelsea, Liverpool, Manchester United and Spurs? They would be carrying the bodies out by lunchtime!

A Freddy Flintoff-inspired Lancashire were the favourites and were promptly knocked out by Gloucestershire in the first semi. Dad and I settled in to watch Kent versus Sussex, then to our dismay saw the Sussex openers smash our bowlers around the ground with a century opening partnership at nearly 10 runs an over. Our optimism was replaced quickly with groans of discontent.

I won't give you a full, blow-by-blow account of the day, but suffice it to say that Kent somehow found a way back against Sussex, winning with two or three balls to spare in the last over.

Miraculously the same happened again in the final. We looked finished during an inspired batting display from Gloucestershire until Ryan McLaren took a hatrick of wickets to disrupt the flow, and again Kent's batsmen got home with a couple of balls to go.

At last we had done it: we had seen Kent win a trophy together. What a day! I can still see the smiling face of the Silver Fox (my dad) as the trophy was lifted. But the best part of that day was just watching Dad's effect on the people around him. He was a magnet; people just warmed to him. In particular, a group of about 15 twentysomethings took him under their wing and we ended up sitting with them for the final. They loved him. 'Your Dad, mate, the Silver Fox, what a legend!' They are words I still savour to this day and that bring a smile to my lips every time I think of them.

As you can see from that back story, it should have been simple: Kent for the cricket with Dad and Chelsea for the football with Grandad. But Grandad (with hindsight) took a slightly risky, in fact reckless approach in his selection of my first game: Chelsea v Liverpool at Stamford Bridge.

I was so excited. I can remember Grandad introducing me to the people who sat around him, in particular three old ladies who were hilarious and looking at him in awe as he took a quick swig from his hip flask.

Then it happened. The players came out to warm up, and although there was no thunder and lightning or angels singing, I did see Kevin Keegan for the first time in the red shirt of Liverpool. (A Charlton Heston style biblical introduction would have given it no more gravitas in my eyes.)

Now for those of you who don't know, at the time Keegan was a legend, a bit like a David Beckham of the 1970s. He was captain of England, he had a hit record and he was regularly on TV. He advertised *Brut* aftershave with the boxer Henry Cooper – 'Splash it all over' was the catch phrase: metrosexual men were still a thing of the future.

Most notably, his famous wobbly cycle ride on *Superstars* resulted in him taking most of the skin off his arms and legs as he came off before the finish line, worth looking at on YouTube.

Superstars was a show that had people from different sports competing against each other for points. Can you imagine a Premier League club releasing, say, Harry Kane to compete in something like that today? The insurance companies would have a fit. I can see it now: Harry, Anthony Joshua, Ben Stokes & Danny Cipriani seeing who could do the most squat thrusts or the best high jump. Bring it back – it would be perfect for Channel 5.

Back to Keegan: to cap it all, he also had an iconic perm hairstyle, which is still synonymous with that time. I guess I have painted you the picture now!

There I was, an impressionable five-year-old, and I uttered the words to my grandad that would change everything: 'Grandad, I want to support the team with Kevin Keegan on it.' It's funny; I don't recall a big argument or debate, or even him trying to convince me to support Chelsea. It just happened, and from that moment to this I have been a Liverpool fan (at the time ticking rule boxes iii and iv) for 40+ years.

I never remember us having a cross word on football. Our relationship was more about how much we loved the game and I always had a soft spot for Chelsea as a result of that. Sadly, that changed long after Grandad had passed away (I'm glad to say), when José Mourinho arrived with the Abramovich millions at Chelsea and a major rivalry commenced with Liverpool as Mourinho and Reds manager Rafael Benítez locked horns in all the cup competitions.

Most famous was the Champions League semi-final in 2005 where red-hot favourites and Premier League champions-elect Chelsea were beaten by what Mourinho called 'The Ghost Goal' from Luis García. Goal-line technology today would have sorted it.

Liverpool went on to win the Champions League that year in Istanbul (more of that later). How myself and my Grandad would have got through that semi-final I don't know. I like to think we would have been okay though: too much love there to fall out.

So, all was straightforward at this point in footballing terms with Liverpool. There were the highs of league titles before the formation of the Premier League (and not won again since 1990: arghhh), FA Cups (most recently in 2006 under Rafa with a Roy of the Rovers-style Steven Gerrard goal against West Ham), and League Cups (our most recent trophy coming against Cardiff City after extra time and penalties in 2012). In Europe, Liverpool have won more UEFA Cups and European Cups/ Champions Leagues than any British club with three and five 5 respectively. Under Gérard Houllier in 2001 came a treble of League Cup, Uefa Cup and FA Cup (the Michael Owen Final, in which we robbed a great Arsenal side).

The lows include missing out on the Premier League title as runners up in 2002 (under Houllier), 2009 (under Benítez) & 2014 (under Brendan Rodgers), and further European Cup or Champions League wins as runners-up to Juventus (1985), AC Milan (2007) and Real Madrid (2018). And of course, at the time of writing we are waiting for Jürgen Klopp to break his run of six losing finals, (three with Liverpool). I'm comforted knowing he is the right man to do it!

I have to say the most painful low of all for me was the first, losing the FA Cup Final in 1977 to our biggest rivals Manchester United. My dislike of them was cemented at that point.

I was buzzing after my favourite player at the time, Jimmy Case, who would also go on to play for Brighton, had turned and smashed an equaliser into the top corner. But we lost to a deflected goal that Brian Greenhoff and Lou Macari both tried to claim. To rub salt, broken glass and hydrochloric acid into the open wound, the defeat also cost us a treble, as we won the European Cup and the Football League title that year. It would also have protected us from the smugness of the United fans that was to come when they won the treble in 1999.

I was eight years old and went down to the shed in the garden and cried my eyes out in front of our rabbit Bumper. Yes, he should have been Thumper, after the one in Bambi, but I couldn't pronounce it. That wasn't my only Bambi embarrassment, as my dad had to carry me out of the cinema after five minutes when Bambi's mum was shot because I was wailing so loudly! I can still feel those warm, bitter tears (the United, not the Bambi ones).

Almost but not quite as bad was Steven Gerrard's slip in a home game against Chelsea that effectively cost Liverpool the Premier League title in 2014, sealed by a capitulation away to Crystal Palace. At least Stevie G admitted to crying in the car all the way home after the Chelsea game. It was important to know that he felt our pain.

I always remember Frank Skinner talking about the way a West Brom defeat would leave him down for days. Then, one evening, he was leaving the pub nearby when some players came out of the ground with their wives, laughing and joking. West Brom had lost that day and Frank was devastated by seeing the players who didn't seem to have a care in the world when he was at rock bottom. Stevie G passed Frank's test with flying colours.

Then the seismic footballing shift happened. We moved from London to Worthing in West Sussex in 2004: myself, Jo, Megan (5) & Jacob (4) with Finlay on the way.

It started so innocently. Brighton, our new local team (tick for rule i), played at Withdean Stadium, originally a temporary home, that they ended up in from 1999 to 2011. It was an athletics track and had an almighty capacity of 8,850!

Brighton's history before that had been mixed. Founded in 1901, their glory period was between 1979 and 1983 when they played in the old first division and also reached the FA Cup Final against Manchester United despite being relegated in the same season. The final was famous for the Brighton team's arrival by helicopter and for their striker Gordon Smith missing a golden chance to win the Cup in the dying seconds. The radio commentator's famous line was 'And Smith Must Score.' But he didn't and Brighton were thumped 4-0 in the replay. Ouch!

The original home ground (The Goldstone) was sold out from under them, to become a retail park. The board responsible, mainly

91

majority shareholder Bill Archer and his chief executive David Bellotti, are still sung about at pretty much every game, and not in complimentary terms as you can imagine. Brighton almost went out of the Football League completely in 1997 and for two seasons had to play their home games at Gillingham 70 miles away before the move to Withdean, where we Clarkes picked up their story.

There were some strong links between Brighton and Liverpool. Michael Robinson and Mark Lawrenson had gone from the Seagulls to the Reds in high-profile deals, Lawrenson being one half of what is widely thought of as their greatest ever centre back partnership along with Alan Hansen. Jimmy Case had gone in the opposite direction as part of the Lawrenson transfer and remains very popular at both clubs.

Withdean was the location for Jacob and Megan's first game, Brighton coming from behind to beat Gillingham 2-1. The female steward jokingly told Jacob (aged four at the time) to stop stamping his feet. His sense of humour hadn't developed at that point and he looked mortified, bordering on tearful. Still, there was a happy ending.

I had already started brainwashing Jacob and Megan with Liverpool and Jacob's next live game was significantly different. We went from about 6,000 at Withdean to Liverpool versus Manchester United at Anfield. We were running late, we parked the car and had to sprint to the ground, then we came up the steps to our seats just as the chorus of *You'll Never Walk Alone* started from the Liverpool supporters. Jacob was overwhelmed: 45,000 people, red and white everywhere. For the first 20 minutes he paid no attention to the football and just looked around the stadium and at the crowd, dumbfounded.

However, brainwashing aside, I always felt I had missed out on having the opportunity of supporting a local team. I went to

Anfield, always saw Liverpool in London, was obsessed with the team, but the one thing I didn't have was being a scouser, a local, which always hit home at London matches when they sang 'Shit on the Cockneys', my mate Vinny (a scouser) singing it as loud as possible next to me with a big grin on his face.

I had amazing experiences at games and was always made to feel welcome, in particular when my wife Jo arranged tickets for a game at Anfield as a birthday present. Vinny (who as well as going to London games with me, was also my boss at work), invited us to share the scouser match day experience. It was brilliant, pub from opening time at 11am, every generation in there, from those not quite old enough to drink through to the grandads who had seen it all. They were magnificent, with incredible stories. What a day, culminating in about eight of us bundling into a Ford Escort to get to the ground. But I still wasn't a local: I couldn't go to the ground and bump into mates. I longed for it, but it was the one hole in my Liverpool experience.

So, I wanted to give my kids that opportunity, and to be honest I wanted to see what it would feel like from my perspective as well. Also there were no conflicts of interest as Liverpool were in the Premier League and Brighton were two divisions below in League One. Things would, of course, change over time ....

Jacob and I started with odd games at Withdean that became more regular, one big highlight being the defeat of Manchester City in the League Cup, just after the billionaire take-over of City. Good old Glenn Murray had scored as usual in normal time and we won after extra time and penalties (at our end). We all invaded the pitch afterwards under the lights: fantastic.

The pivotal moment was when Gus Poyet took over as manager. The former Uruguay, Chelsea and Spurs midfield player galvanised the club. He came in 2009, saved us from relegation from League

One and then took us up as Champions into the Championship in 2011.

In parallel, local businessman and fan Tony Bloom had taken over the club after agreeing to finance a new ground at Falmer. After a number of planning enquiries, the Labour government's Communities Secretary, Hazel Blears, had given the stadium the final green light in 2007 and it was confirmed that we would start to play our home games there from the 2011-12 season.

The capacity would be 22,000, with expansion plans agreed to take it to 30,000. This was the promised land, Brighton as a Premier League club in the making, an observation that would be made many times over in relation to Brighton over the coming years.

I decided to place the ultimate test on Jacob as to whether he was ready to dedicate himself to the Albion and to take it to the next level with a season ticket. Brighton were offering one from November that would also then get you onto the waiting list for the Amex (short for the American Express Community Stadium), our new ground.

The challenge was simple. Prove that you can sit in Withdean's temporary uncovered seats from November through to early May in the rain, wind and snow, maintain your attendance (every home game is a significant step up) and then, my son, you will be ordained at the end of the season with a season ticket for the new ground.

Gus Poyet's team helped to soften the impact of the weather with some fantastic performances and really entertaining games. Captained by Gordon Greer, with a front line of Murray, Ashley Barnes and Chris Wood (the latter two now at Burnley in the Premier League) and with even some very early sightings of future vice-captain Lewis Dunk, Brighton were crowned champions, beating Southampton to the title, who included now future

Liverpool and England regulars Adam Lallana and Alexander Oxlade Chamberlain.

We were arriving at our new stadium as a Championship side, only one step away from the Premier League. Five years later we would be there after three failed play off attempts under Poyet, Óscar García and Hughton. It was to be Hughton who finally took us to our Nirvana moment.

However, this complicated my situation. Suddenly I was in new territory: Liverpool and Brighton in the same division. Can you love two women, a wife and a mistress? Can you support two teams in the same division? Liverpool, a team I had supported from the age of five for around 45 years, and Brighton, local and where I was a season ticket holder, and whom I had supported for 14 years.

Up to this point I had received the odd piece of stick for having two teams: 'Oh Kev, who you supporting this week then? Are you gonna support Worthing as well?' (Jacob was playing U18's football there, but three teams is taking the piss and is logistically virtually impossible – and that is without the legal costs of a certain divorce.)

Brighton had drawn Liverpool in the League Cup at the Amex in their first season at the new place, which again brought it to a head, but my way of thinking was simple; that 45 years plays 14.

But once Brighton hit the Premier League, then I was fair game in any footballing debate. In particular on social media, just as I would use the five European Cups as my closing comment to dig the knife into Manchester United fans in particular, I was now on the receiving end of any variant on the two teams theme as a perceived knockout blow.

Worse than that though, there was an undercurrent of bitterness to Brighton's success as they made it to the Premier League. It was all right supporting them when they were in League One or the

Championship and knew their place, but not now. It came mainly from mates who were Fulham fans, still upset, I think, that they hadn't become 'The Manchester United of the South' as then chairman Mohamed al Fayed had predicted.

'When did you start supporting them?' 'You jumped on the bandwagon' (what, at Withdean?); 'Oh Brighton, they are everyone's favourite second team' et cetera.

So, I exist in a sort of barren footballing landscape. On the one side the Liverpool fans, where you have the missing link of not being a scouser, plus the added abuse of not supporting a local team from your London mates. On the other the Brighton fans, knowing they are a very close second behind Liverpool, and not having the full history, having only dedicated 14 years rather than 45. That is the football politics that I need to navigate through, 'normal' to every true football fan out there, to others very odd.

Don't feel sorry for me, though. It has not dampened my enjoyment or love of the game. This unique position has, in fact, added to both the banter and the intensity of wins and losses. This is why we are in it, after all – that incredible high when your team scores a crucial goal and you are ready to hug anyone in a reasonably close vicinity, or that gut-wrenching ache after a defeat or conceding late on.

What I can tell you is that what I thought impossible is not. You *can* support two teams.

There, I said it.

Don't hate me. It could happen to you. Seriously, it really could! It's all about the emotional attachment that generates those feelings explained above. I have that with both Liverpool and Brighton, the Liverpool commitment over a lifetime and the Brighton one, now much more regular as a season ticket holder.

The aspirations are different, trophies versus staying in the Premier League, but both are equally enjoyable. It's like watching my sons play football, Jacob the older one has always played to a decent standard and has won trophies playing in the top divisions locally and is now starting in county football. Fin's teams have played at a lower standard and wins and trophies are rarer. But I can honestly say that I get equal pleasure from both.

So in my self-imposed rule book I've never hit points i and ii - sorry again Grandad, but iii and iv are a yes all day long. A Liver Bird and a Seagull.

So that leaves the final question, doesn't it? The one that I get asked all the time.

It's my small-time version of Noel and Liam Gallagher being asked whether Oasis will ever get back together. Or Tony Blair and Gordon Brown if there really was a gentlemen's agreement struck at the Granita restaurant in Islington that Blair would stand down after two terms and pass the leadership of the country on to Brown.

'So, Kevin – who are you supporting today: Liverpool or Brighton?'

The answer? Well, again the simple version is '45 years versus 14, what do you think?' But as always the devil is in the detail; circumstances could also have an impact.

Imagine if Brighton needed to win to stay up and Liverpool at the time were safely in a Champions League spot? Or imagine – no, there are so many combinations and I'm sure you can work them out without me taking you through another six paragraphs on the scenarios.

So as per the title graphics on this book, I'm Red, Blue & White and I'm not apologising anymore!

98

A 49th birthday present from Megan's boyfriend depicting my football schizophrenia

Frederick Ernest Eason – also known as Peter or Grandad!

Mum, Dad, Tracy & Kevin

12.   Dads & Daughters

'My Confession' in the previous chapter, as well as being a cathartic experience, also allows me to talk about women in football, in particular my daughter Megan, who has had a significant role to play in footballing terms. There have been various stages where her interest, knowledge and enthusiasm for the sport has peaked and troughed.

Megan has felt my pain and excitement and has also been disillusioned and completely uninterested. Liverpool does figure quite prominently along the way, so the timing of this introduction had to be laser sharp (well after the 'confession' chapter anyway).

Megan was born in 1999, so at the age of six in 2005 thought her Dad was the best thing in the world: handsome, funny, intelligent, you name it – it was all there before she developed a mind of her own!

We had just moved to Worthing the year before, but in footballing history 2005 was to contain the greatest moment in my life. Rafa Benítez, in his first season as coach of a team captained by Liverpool legend Steven Gerrard, won the Champions League in Istanbul in what is widely regarded as the greatest final ever. Liverpool came back from 3-0 down at half time to score three goals in seven history-making minutes of the second half before going on to win on penalties after extra time, courtesy of Polish keeper Jerzy Dudek.

As a result of this momentous event, Megan knew all the songs thanks to an excellent brain washing job from me, and we sang them regularly together, much to my wife Jo's irritation. The following had numerous repeat choruses:

'We won it five times, we won it five times; in Istanbul we won it five times;'

'Rafa, Rafael, Rafa, Rafael, Rafa, Rafael, Rafael Benítez;'

'Luis García, he drinks sangria, he came from Barca, to bring us joy, he's four-foot seven, he's football heaven, oh don't take our Luis away.'

Are you irritated yet?

We then started to go to Brighton as I wanted the kids to have a local team as per the last chapter, so all was good: supporting Liverpool for Dad and Brighton as the family deal in our new home.

Then Megan hit her teenage years and this wonderful equilibrium was thrown up into the air as she decided she was supporting Chelsea (knowing full well that Manchester United and Chelsea were the teams I detested the most – I think even she knew in her teenage haze that United would have been a step too far!).

Megan had her own mind after all (damn!) and Chelsea were Liverpool's main rivals in the cups during this period, so our footballing relationship became tense, particularly as Jacob and Finlay were on board with Liverpool along with Brighton.

Ironically it took one of my all-time footballing lows to bring Megan back to me, the Brendan Rodgers-led Liverpool charge towards the holy grail of the Premier League title. This was totally unexpected as we had finished eighth the year prior to Rodgers joining from Swansea. In his first season we improved by a place into 7th, then came season 2013-14, never to be forgotten.

To be fair, he was very ambitious. He had learnt to speak fluent Spanish for future international assignments and whilst at Liverpool lost a fair chunk of weight and had his teeth whitened. Liverpool was referred to as 'a project,' so the modern manager was born. My mate Tim likened him to David Brent, played by Ricky Gervais in the TV show *The Office* after watching an ill-advised documentary on his first season in charge.

The team were a delight to watch, with a dynamic front line of Luis Suárez, Daniel Sturridge and Raheem Sterling. They scored four in the first half at home to Arsenal, who had the best defence in the league at the time: still one of the best 45 minutes I have seen from any Liverpool side over the years. They scored 101 goals by the end of the season, the most the club had managed for nearly 120 years! (1895-96 for those who like the detail). For the sake of balance we also conceded 50: ouch!

The title run in was a head-to-head with the billionaires of Manchester City. Each match was an emotional roller-coaster, which I struggled to handle at times, as demonstrated by an event in my front room that caused much amusement for my kids at the time and is still talked about to this day.

It happened at the end of the victory against Norwich at Anfield, another step closer to the title. Gerrard had the team in a huddle telling them how we mustn't let this slip – those words still hurt as I type them – but there was I, after a few beers it must be said, looking down on the telly as if to get a better view of what was going on inside that huddle and listen to Stevie!

Megan saw how much it meant to her dad, the emotional toll of these games after years of failed attempts. Before every match there were the Liverpool flags, red smoke bombs and an army of supporters surrounding the team coaches miles from the ground. Megan became desperate for Liverpool to make it on my behalf. This was the moment that we thought would never come again – and it didn't.

That lowest of the low footballing moment happened against Chelsea – it would be, wouldn't it? – as Stevie Gerrard, our idol and Champions League winner, slipped at the crucial moment, allowing Chelsea's Demba Ba to step in, take the ball and comfortably slot it under the body of Liverpool goalkeeper Simon Mignolet.

There is a song that I won't repeat that was sung to Gerrard at every Premier League ground after that until he retired. Manchester United, Chelsea and Everton fans still sing it now, even when he is nowhere to be seen, as they know it's like a dagger to Liverpool hearts.

That was the moment – forget the 3-3 draw against Palace that was to follow – this was when it went out of our hands. And against a Mourinho-led, anti-football, seven-at-the-back Chelsea team, that, to rub salt in the wounds, also included former Liverpool legend Fernando Torres. Arrrggghhhhhh!!!

Megan felt my pain. She was there for me when I needed her, and suddenly it was as if that teenage demonstration of independence had never happened. Megan as a Chelsea fan was consigned to Room 101 for evermore.

Myself and Megan then moved onto our second footballing phase, watching Brighton at the Amex Stadium together. I have to be honest: this had a non footballing hook for her, which I eventually twigged!

I started going to the games with the Taylor brothers after an introduction from a mutual friend. There are six of them, seven originally, all Brighton fans who grew up in the area, most of whom now run bars or restaurants around Worthing. They are a sort of middle class Kray firm, more likely to put a skinny latte in your face than a glass. Maybe the exception was Andy, who was to become a close mate. His fuse can be pretty short, but he will still be very articulate before giving you a slap!

The Taylor boys introduced me to middle class football. We used to meet at Stanmer House, a Grade 1 listed mansion with a restaurant, before home games, the main reason being that you could park there and then walk to the Amex. It was the full Taylor entourage, plus friends, kids, cousins et cetera. Jacob and I were quickly indoctrinated (Fin was old school – he preferred a pie at the ground and I will come to Megan in a moment).

We got used to a quality meal and good wine, with plenty of football debate amongst other things, Jacob playing outside with the other boys, although it couldn't last, of course, as our bank accounts couldn't take it!

But during this time, when I took Megan to a game (we had two tickets so I alternated between the three kids), she was hooked on Stanmer. So I would book a table for two, where I got quality time with my beautiful teenage daughter, getting to have proper chats about what was really going on in her life – well, the bits she wanted to tell me anyway. And in return, she got to eat very well, which was top of her agenda during our time together.

Once in the ground you felt that the main event had already passed for Megan. Her mobile phone was out and dominated the possession stats Pep-stylie. Although she did always find time to join in with the goal celebrations (and I mean join in! She was full on for that – Megs does like to win).

Megan also enjoyed the rants from Mr Pimples, who sat next to me. Now let me be clear: Mr Pimples is quality. I feel terrible about the nickname. I think one of the kids dished it out as he has a skin condition. It wasn't done nastily, more as a reference to who they were talking about when they originally saw him and, more importantly, heard him.

I'm sure the seats became available next to him because the previous occupants wanted a move as they didn't enjoy the verbal tirades dished out by him, which we grew to love. Their fickle nature was our bonus as we got great seats and great entertainment off the pitch as well as on.

The first thing you need to know about Mr Pimples (it's with horror that after about six years of sitting next to him, I've just realised I don't know his real name even though we talk at every game – oh dear) is that he hates all referees with a passion. He normally asks someone who has a programme who the ref is before the game so that his insults can be more personal.

He also has a habit of getting so wound up in the emotion of the game that when he is particularly riled, the words won't get out as fast as his brain is thinking of them – a classic being when we were managed by Sami Hyppia, the former Finland Captain, Liverpool legend and Champions League winner, who turned out to be a disaster for Brighton and almost got us relegated.

Mr Pimples was not happy as he screamed 'You ... you ... you ...' – (getting redder and redder and about to spontaneously combust) ' ... Finnish Muppet!' at the top of his voice. That was the kids' all-time favourite. There have been many more. I have also had to prevent him from spinning a full 360 degrees and falling into the row in front (I think that one was a goal celebration).

Finally, Megan's other contribution (when looking up from her phone) was to dish it out to our players if they were not putting in enough effort. 'They are so weak. They need to man up, Dad' being a particular favourite, which seemed even more damning somehow coming out of the mouth of a teenage girl.

The dad and daughter footy journey now has our equivalent of a winter break as Megan heads off to university in Edinburgh. Has the journey come to an end? Not sure. I will know more in four years' time.

13.   Jo

My wife Jo is the dealmaker in this transaction, or, more accurately, the only person with the power of veto. There she stood like a seasoned United Nations member, fingers drumming on the table looking down at me, knowing that the financial and emotional impact along with the investment of time into this adventure, all had to be rubber-stamped by her.

I looked deep into Jo's eyes and was reminded of Clint Eastwood in the movie Dirty Harry – 'You've got to ask yourself a question: "Do I feel lucky?" Well, do ya, punk?' I wasn't sure how lucky I felt, but it did dawn on me in that moment that Jo and the footballing gods didn't always play nicely together.

To elaborate and for additional context, we need to go back to when I met my wife Jo, in November 1991. Liverpool had won the league title (the pre-Premier League first division) in 1990. I was not to know that from that day until this in 2018, that we would never have won it since, during our entire relationship including 25 years of marriage.

Now, I'm not sure I can blame Jo entirely for the failure of successive Liverpool managers to lift the coveted Premier League crown, but I have to say that she did mislead me on the football front in the early part of our relationship. Oh yes, Jo hooked me and reeled me in.

When I met her in '91, it was at the salubrious location of Cinatra's (yes, it was spelt like that) night club in Croydon. It was obviously meant to be, as we both had unusual routes to being there that night.

I was with a group of mates leaving the local pub when a heated debate commenced about whether we should go to Cinatra's or Le Palais in Hammersmith (basically the old Hammersmith Palais, where, incidentally, my mum and dad met. He had holes in his shoes but was taller than Mum, so he warranted a dance at least).

I was fed up with Cinatra's, and with just cause: let me paint a picture for you. You had to be suited and booted to get in, at a fixed cost of about £15 and you got all your food and drink for free. They laid on a beautiful cold buffet table, 70s wedding-style: sausage rolls, ham, French bread, crisps, nuts. I'm sure the ladies really appreciated being approached by a guy wasted on 'free' booze, emitting hot breath with an aroma of stale sausage rolls along with a tongue pebble-dashed with dry roasted peanuts.

The young guys had to be on the lookout as well, as the place was renowned for an older, more experienced group of women, usually divorcees who would prey on the fresh meat. The usual routine was to grab the unsuspecting victim's arse, whisk him onto the dance floor, followed by some very suggestive moves, before he was taken upstairs to what was locally known as 'BJ Corner' - a dimly-lit area of burgundy armchairs and sofas, where all sorts of sexual activity took place. Primarily blowjobs (hence the name, for those of you who hadn't worked it out already), while the bouncers turned a blind eye, no doubt also identifying personal targets for the following week.

Still dizzy from the experience and slightly weakened both mentally and physically, the individual would then find themselves in a taxi going back to her place. At this point I will spare you from the sordid details. It was a bit like the beginning of the famous American TV series *Roots,* written by Alex Haley, in which Kunta Kinte went into the jungle as a boy and came out a man. What Kunta didn't have to deal with was waking up the next morning with an unrecognisable woman next to him and screaming children in the bedroom next door. Suddenly the previous night's events would seem a distant memory, replaced with 'Shit, where am I and how do I get home from here?'

Cinatra's also had an incredibly sticky carpet (and not just around BJ Corner, I might add). To get to the dance floor, it felt like you were walking in quicksand or that you had trodden on an entire packet of Wrigley's Juicy Fruits. Basically it was the sort of place where you wiped your feet on the way out.

Its final endearing feature was that some of the Christmas decorations stayed up all year round and there were netted balloons above the dance floor gathering dust. I think they were only released every New Year's Eve. Unless you had your anti-histamine on you, it was time to run for cover.

What a place. So, as I'm sure you have guessed, I lost the argument with my mates and ended up in there.

What was Jo, my future wife, doing in such an establishment you may ask? Well she was invited to a Hen Party by a friend (she didn't even know the girl getting married). They had dinner in Croydon and, not wanting to go home afterwards, someone made the suggestion that was to change Jo's life forever: 'What about Cinatra's? It's only down the road!'

Ok, I've digressed (again). So in those early stages of our relationship, Jo hooked me beautifully with the line: 'I'm not really into football, but I do like going to live games.' She has backed that up once, by getting me tickets for Liverpool v Wimbledon at Anfield for my birthday, which she attended as well (our scouse experience already captured elsewhere in this book).

I should mention that this was before we got married, so 25 years have followed with, I think, ONE trip to the Amex for Brighton versus Nottingham Forest (supposedly her home-town team). If I recall correctly, she spent around 80 of the 90 minutes consulting her mobile phone in detail. I would have brought her a couple of magazines and a nail file if I'd realised.

Fair play to Jo, though: she has put up with a lot of football-related social activity over the years and has had to deal with my moods, ranging from wild hysteria to clinical depression. And I mustn't forget that our 19 away trips wouldn't have happened without us signing up to a sort of footy ten-month pre-nuptial agreement.

Jo has also learnt to curb the more acidic and condescending comments directed at me, that usually followed horrific defeats to late injury-time goals and caused me to spontaneously combust, such as:

'Come on; it's only a game of football' – treating me like an 11 year old boy.

'You didn't really expect them to win did you?' – making me feel like an 11 year old boy

'When will you learn? They never end up winning anything' – ditto both of the above

My beautiful wife Jo, intelligent, funny and wonderful in so many ways, but a football philistine!

14.   Rivalry

Rivalry is huge in football. After all, the sport and its fans thrive on the tribalism.   The stakes are higher, the pressure greater, the adrenalin rush of winning is astronomic and the lows of defeat catastrophic, with not just weekends, but whole weeks and months, spoilt as a result.   Until you get your opportunity for revenge, of course.

This is international in scope as well, see below for a list of the biggest in the world from Argentina, to Italy, to Scotland, all significant and historic in their own right.

Real Madrid v Barcelona (El Clasico)

AC Milan v Inter Milan (Derby della Madonnina)

Liverpool v Manchester United (The North West Derby)

Manchester United v Manchester City (The Manchester Derby)

Boca Juniors v River Plate (Super Clasico)

Bayern Munich v Borussia Dortmund (Der Klassiker)

Arsenal v Spurs (The North London Derby)

Real Madrid v Atletico Madrid (El Derbi Madrileno)

Liverpool v Everton (The Merseyside Derby)

Rangers v Celtic (The Old firm Derby)

Ajax v PSV (De Topper)

Lazio v Roma (Derby Del Sole)

The list goes on and on...

But, I hear you all shout in unison, where on this line up is Brighton v Crystal Palace? This "Derby" is intriguing ... I have to say that in my London year's pre the south coast move, I was blissfully unaware that this rivalry even existed, and I know I'm not alone. It has gained more prominence in the press in recent years since the two sides met in the play-offs to get into the Premier League (in 2013, when Palace were successful). And now, of course, in Brighton's first season in the Premier League, a top flight meeting would take place for the first time in 36 years.

So how did this mutual dislike come about? Let me give the uninitiated a top level briefing on the back story, before bringing us back to the 2017-18 season.

The clubs are 45 miles apart and the tale of their intense rivalry dates back to 1976...(imagine a wobbly picture frame now as we look back). Picture the UK heatwave, getting water from outside taps, John Curry becoming an Olympic gold medalist in ice skating, a Eurovision song contest win from Brotherhood of Man with Save All Your Kisses for Me, Harold Wilson (Labour Prime Minister) and Jeremy Thorpe (Leader of the Liberal Party) both resigning, the trial of "The Black Panther" Donald Nielson begins, the first punk single is released (New Rose by The Damned), Agatha Christie passes away and Terry Venables becomes Crystal Palace manager as does Alan Mullery down at Brighton.

Venables and Mullery had spent time together on the field as players at Spurs, and Venables was second in command to Mullery's captaincy at the club; Mullery has described this power dynamic as a reason for the antagonism between them.

Whilst at Spurs, Venables reportedly did not have a good relationship with his manager Bill Nicholson, believing him to have a negative attitude that; 'drained him of enthusiasm'. Venables also felt that he was not appreciated by the Spurs fans, in contrast to Mullery, who was Nicholson's and the fans' favourite.

The two young managers were set the same target at their respective clubs: promotion from the Third Division.

The first meeting between Palace and Brighton that season was the league match which ended 1–1; during the game, smoke bombs were thrown onto the pitch and play was stopped three times. The clubs were then drawn together in the first round of the FA Cup, at The Goldstone; the match ended 2–2. After the game, Mullery was critical of his opposite number, bemoaning what he perceived to be Palace's negative tactics.

A replay took place at Selhurst Park three days later; the match finished 1–1 after extra time and the teams faced a second replay. Incredibly both matches attracted crowds of almost 30,000. This attendance figure was a significant increase on both club's averages for the season, with Palace averaging just 15,925 that season and Brighton 20,197.

The second replay, postponed twice due to bad weather, took place at Stamford Bridge (Chelsea's ground) on December 6th. Palace took the lead after 18 minutes through Phil Holder. Brighton dominated much of the remainder of the game, with striker Peter Ward having a goal disallowed shortly after as he was judged to have handled the ball, although Palace's Jim Cannon later said that this only occurred due to him shoving the Brighton striker.

In the 78th minute, Brighton were awarded a penalty which was converted by Brian Horton only to be disallowed as referee Ron Challis ruled that players had encroached upon the penalty area. Horton retook the penalty and this time it was saved by the Palace keeper, Paul Hammond. The match ended 1–0 to Crystal Palace.

After the final whistle, Mullery approached Challis to discuss the decision and was escorted off the pitch by police while flicking 'v-signs' and swearing at the Palace supporters in the stands.

Afterwards, Mullery claims he had a cup of boiling hot coffee poured on him by Palace fans. The Brighton manager then allegedly entered the Palace dressing room, threw five pounds on the floor and told Venables: 'Your team's not worth that'. Mullery was fined £100 by the Football Association for bringing the game into disrepute.

The two sides met again in the league at Selhurst and Palace ran out 3–1 winners. A crowd of 28,808, nearly double Palace's average for the season, was present, the rivalry clearly now in full swing.

That season both teams were promoted, with Brighton finishing as runners up, two points in front of Palace. Brighton also changed their official nickname from the Dolphins to the Seagulls, in a direct echo of the Crystal Palace nickname, the Eagles.

The conflict continued with the clubs meeting with the same objective and same managers in both the 1977-78 and 1978-79 seasons, this time vying for a spot in the top flight of English football.

In 1978, Brighton missed out on promotion on goal difference, finishing in fourth place and well ahead of Crystal Palace in ninth.

Brighton completed their 1978-79 campaign on top of the table. Palace, though, still had a game in hand to play against Burnley due to postponements throughout the season; Palace won the match, played in front of 51,000 spectators, and took the title by one point. For the second time in three years, the two clubs had been promoted together.

Mullery states that the rivalry was fueled by both competition between the teams and directly between the managers. Terry Venables, highly controversially, left Palace in 1980 for Queens Park Rangers while Alan Mullery left Brighton in 1981.

Both clubs were relegated from the first division within a few years, Palace in 1981 and Brighton in 1983. The two years that Brighton spent above Palace from 1981 to 1983 have since been the only years that Brighton have competed in a higher league than Crystal Palace.

Mullery went on to manage Crystal Palace for two seasons (1982–1984 – the irony!) and then returned to Brighton in the late eighties. Venables of course went on to manage Barcelona and then England, famously taking them to the semi-finals at Euro 96, when our current England manager Gareth Southgate, also an ex Palace captain, missed his penalty (I feel his moment of retribution will come – let's hope so...).

Even more recently there have been incidents. When the Eagles knocked Brighton out of the Championship play-offs on their way to sealing promotion to the Premier League in 2013, they were greeted before the game with an unsavoury gift in their dressing room - excrement smeared over the floor. Palace defender Paddy McCarthy later suggested that their coach driver had been responsible, but I won't get into the details of the accused on that one – I can't afford a libel action! Needless to say, it is now referred to as 'Poo-Gate'.

The first Premier League meeting between Brighton and Palace finally took place at The Amex in 2017-18. It ended uneventfully on the pitch, 0-0. But away from the action, there was crowd trouble outside the ground which resulted in several stewards from both clubs suffering minor injuries. Ticketless Palace fans stormed the turnstiles, pyrotechnics were let off at the away end and the police closed the entrances six minutes into the match, leaving many unhappy fans with tickets outside.

So, I hope you found that history lesson helpful to contextualise this huge match which should be added to the dozen listed previously from around the world, often now branded as the M23 Derby. It is incredible what a fixture list and some management fall-outs can create between clubs.

Look at Liverpool versus Chelsea, another example of a rivalry that has grown up in relatively recent times. It all stemmed from a series of Champions League and domestic cup games and a mutual dislike between managers Rafa Benitez and Jose Mourinho, proving that new rivalries can still be created.

That sets us up nicely for our finish, doesn't it? What better away match to end on in this book than the M23 Derby? I wouldn't have been forgiven by Brighton fans for not dedicating at least a chapter to this historic encounter.

Unfortunately I'm struggling for positives. It was the first game in the Premier League that season to have five goals in the first half, but unfortunately three of them went to Palace. No more goals were to be added, and sadly Glenn Murray missed a great chance late on to seal a draw against his former club but it wasn't to be. Zaha scored two more against Brighton; that's five now, more than he has scored against any other club. He's starting to love this derby more than us!

The atmosphere was fantastic, smoke bombs somehow smuggled in as a response to the Palace firework display at the Amex, but thankfully no trouble. The arrival of the Palace players at the ground was old school which I liked as they walked through a tunnel of Palace fans shaking hands with everyone. It was like the old days and portrayed a much closer bond between fans and players that was welcomed.

Just behind Murray's miss, the Palace victory and myself and Jacob's failed Grand National bets in reasons to forget the day was the exit from Selhurst Park. This was at the opposite end of the scale from the beautifully-orchestrated mass exodus at West Ham, albeit with the help of the Hammers fans.

We left the ground to return to the car, only to be escorted in the opposite direction and then held indefinitely by the Police 'for our own safety', kettling in action. However, there was a golden ticket out of this mess, which was proof that you were on one of the away coaches. Sadly for us we had driven, so the good old parking app was now proving to be a hindrance again.

Many fans did manage to escape before the police got properly organised using the football fan classic of the front person having a ticket and everyone else marching through behind confirming verbally that they did as well.

Jacob and I had missed our moment and were now confronted by row upon row of Sir Robert Peel's finest bobbies, who appeared to be more unhappy than we were to be in this position. I tried humour to break the collective expression on their faces, attempting to register some minor understanding of our predicament, to no avail.

I then moved along the row trying different individuals, but all I got was 'Sorry, we have been told to keep you here'; 'I don't know why'; 'I don't know for how long'; and the killer final line, 'When you are out, we will march you to the opposite side of town' (opposite, that is, to where our car was parked).

Is our entire away journey going to be defined by our parking app, I thought to myself? I was about to give up, then I thought about all those fatherly chats I had with the children: keep trying, don't give up, do the best you can do.

I wheeled out my story again, the parking story told so often, but this time with the added tone of despair, the hope that common sense could prevail, reaching out for empathy. Then I saw it briefly, fleetingly, a minor twitch, a slight brightness in the eyes. This young policeman in front of me was actually processing the information that I had delivered in my impassioned speech.

It was like the scene in the movie Awakenings when Robert De Niro starts to stir for the first time as he comes out of his semi-catatonic state, being released from his coma by courtesy of Robin Williams. He was now speaking to me.

It was like slow motion, almost sounding like a satanic chant: 'Do you have any proof of where you have parked?' I thought for a moment. 'Yes, Yes, Yes,' I shouted a bit too loudly and definitely too hysterically. I could feel many sets of eyes scrutinising my every move now as I fumbled with my iPhone 6, having to catch it once to prevent it from disintegrating into pieces on the pavement in front of my eyes. I loaded my app and there it was. My car had never looked so beautiful, on this wonderful parking application.

I could feel myself welling up as he stepped aside. 'Free at last, free at last, great God a-mighty, we are free at last.' Still gotta get through Croydon though ...

15.   The End

So, what happened?

Well, let's start with my personal stats. 37 out of 38 premier league games attended. I have mentioned the work clash that kept me from the Spurs home game, but I can still hear the groans: 'One game short - how did you let that happen?'

I went into this naively, thinking that if I was committed and determined then the goal could be reached. But then I spoke to my mate Dave, a Chelsea fan who is the only person I know who has achieved 100 percent attendance over a season.

Dave disappointed me on two levels, first informing me that this was in fact not all within my control. What about the weather, train delays, traffic jams, kick off times moving for TV or other teams' European commitments? Road closures, illness, bereavements, birthdays, weddings, funerals, anniversaries, holidays and stag dos? The list was endless; he only left out natural disasters and declarations of war.

He had dampened down my enthusiasm so much at this point that I was now looking at him like a small child who had just started a new school and had been told off in front of the class. Even when I thought it was over, Dave then followed up with a virtual kick in the nuts as he told me that Premier League games weren't enough. 'What do you mean you haven't included the cup games? That doesn't count then.'

My silence was deafening and told him everything. I now had the look of Paul Gascoigne just after he got his yellow card in the World Cup semi-final against Germany in 1990 and realised that if England made it to the final, he wouldn't play. My bottom lip was wobbling, a slight dribble beginning, and there was no Gary Lineker to re-focus me, the bastard.

My mind drifted as I tried to compute this new information. Wondering to myself if Dave had ever considered a role as a motivational speaker. Then I thought: 'This is karma,' as I recalled a similar situation a few years prior with Dave. I had a mobile sales team in BT, Dave was part of it and we had a sales conference coming up where the fancy dress theme for the evening was 80s icons.

I was going as Adam Ant, which I thought was highly original until I bumped into about five other Adams within 15 minutes of arriving. At least I redeemed myself (in my own eyes) by winning the Prince Charming dance-off that occurred later that evening! The team were going as the cast from Scooby Doo, with Nick drawing the short straw as the dog and as a consequence sweating his bollocks off all night.

From the outset Dave had insisted that he was going solo. He had his own idea that he kept secret from all of us, also making it clear to anyone who would listen that he was even making his own outfit.

Fast forward to Friday evening, the end of the working week and Dave and I were catching up: work, footy and the sales conference (which was now imminent) amongst other things. Dave gloated about his homemade outfit, the smugness oozing down the phone line as he basked in the glory of his inspired choice. We had all made many guesses over the preceding weeks and then suddenly out of nowhere I said: 'It isn't Hong Kong Phooey, is it?' (A cartoon character from the 70s/80s for those in the wrong age demographic). And there it was - that same deathly silence that I was to experience years later around my Brighton fixture challenge,

Dave being rendered speechless, making it clear that his secret was no more. I can't repeat what he said next.

So one game missed. Dave was right all along, which was not surprising for a man whose attention to detail resulted in him personally making and sewing on his Hong Kong Phooey ears (he was a dog that did Kung Fu – the cartoon character, not Dave).

However, on a more positive note, the main objective of attending all 19 away games with Jacob was met. It was meant to be; even the finish was perfect, with the last fixture being at Anfield, home of Liverpool, on the final day of the season - Brighton already safe from relegation, Liverpool winning to secure their place in the following season's Champions League and Mo Salah scoring his 32nd goal of the season to set a new Premier League record.

Timing is everything. Jacob was 17, pre legal drinking, he had split up with his girlfriend a couple of months before and there was the general excitement of Brighton being in the Premier League for the first time - the perfect storm. I knew that this was the moment, and the only chance of us doing this together.

Brighton finished in a very respectable 15th place, beating Manchester United at home to achieve 40 points and safety in the Premier League. It couldn't have been sweeter and I couldn't have handpicked the opposition any better.

What a journey: 19 matches, nearly 7,000 miles, 120 hours in the car and ironically, even though we stayed up, our away form was appalling. Out of our 40 points won, only 11 were away from home and we had the dismal record of scoring only ten goals in those 19 games, three of them in one game at West Ham, while conceding 29. Two wins, five draws and 12 losses.

But none of that mattered. I had had 19 road trips with my son. From Bournemouth to Burnley, West Ham to West Brom, Liverpool,

United, City, Chelsea, Arsenal, Spurs at Wembley and of course the much-derided Palace at Selhurst Park.

I wouldn't change any of it: Jacob banging out his Spotify tunes on journeys home, the frustration of traffic jams and defeats, the joy of a goal or a single point, the singing, the dissecting of tactics and players, the sleepovers, the entertaining guests who joined us in the car along the way, the backdrop of talkSPORT, the surprise spotting of Wilfried Zaha coming out of the barbers a couple of hours before the game at Selhurst in full Palace track suit. I could go on and on.

If you love football and you have kids, give it a go, just once. Trust me, it's worth it.

Leicester away - first of the season

Sir John Hall ex Newcastle chairman

'Uncle Dan'

19 and out – Liverpool away

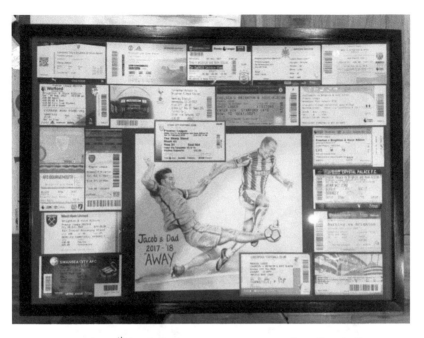

Jacob's 18th birthday present courtesy of Nadia Chalk

(Note the Dunk 'tackle' on Charlie Adam)

Teenager on the road

16.   Epilogue

Megan has just started university in Edinburgh, the first one to leave home. I never cease to be amazed by her determination, confidence and drive.

Jo and I have just celebrated 25 years of marriage, and we both agree that if it all ended tomorrow, we would be grateful for the wonderful years we have had and the family we have created.

Finlay is now a proper teenager with some attitude. He has told me he wants to be a butler or a circus ringmaster, his constantly evolving mind and creativity is something to behold, and he does all this whilst listening to Korean Pop!

Jacob is approaching 18, one month away as I write this. He has a part-time job, is in the final year of A levels and has just passed his driving theory exam with a test to follow soon. The new season has started; we watched a couple of games in a bar in Spain, drinking beers together for the first time.

He is going to Southampton away next week. With his mates. We had our time, now it's his. As Jo's Nan Edith used to say, 'Leave 'em alone and they'll come home…'

Where football's concerned, maybe Al Pacino as Michael Corleone in Godfather Part III is more apt, giving me hope for the future: 'Just when I thought I was out, they pull me back in.'

So, are you a football fan? Are you a **true** football fan?

Having a team isn't enough.

Do you feel physical, gut-wrenching pain when your team loses?

Does a last-minute winning goal render you incapable of controlling body and mind as you spiral into an ecstasy normally only reserved for carnal pleasure or substance abuse?

Do you go AWAY?

17. Appendix A – Brighton Fixtures 2017-18

Date	Home (H) or Away (A)	Opponent	Result
12.08.17	H	Manchester City	0-2
19.08.17	A	Leicester City	0-2
26.08.17	A	Watford	0-0
09.09.17	H	West Bromwich Albion	3-1
15.09.17	A	AFC Bournemouth	1-2
24.09.17	H	Newcastle United	1-0
01.10.17	A	Arsenal	0-2
15.10.17	H	Everton	1-1
20.10.17	A	West Ham United	3-0
29.10.17	H	Southampton	1-1
04.11.17	A	Swansea City	1-0
20.11.17	H	Stoke City	2-2
25.11.17	A	Manchester United	0-1
28.11.17	H	Crystal Palace	0-0
02.12.17	H	Liverpool	1-5
09.12.17	A	Huddersfield Town	0-2
13.12.17	A	Tottenham Hotspur	0-2
16.12.17	H	Burnley	0-0
23.12.17	H	Watford	1-0

Date	Home (H) or Away (A)	Opponent	Result
26.12.17	A	Chelsea	0-2
30.12.17	A	Newcastle United	0-0
01.01.18	H	AFC Bournemouth	2-2
13.01.18	A	West Bromwich Albion	0-2
20.01.18	H	Chelsea	0-4
31.01.18	A	Southampton	1-1
03.02.18	H	West Ham United	3-1
10.02.18	A	Stoke City	1-1
24.02.18	H	Swansea City	4-1
04.03.18	H	Arsenal	2-1
10.03.18	A	Everton	0-2
31.03.18	H	Leicester City	0-2
07.04.18	H	Huddersfield Town	1-1
14.04.18	A	Crystal Palace	2-3
17.04.18	H	Tottenham Hotspur	1-1
28.04.18	A	Burnley	0-0
04.05.18	H	Manchester United	1-0
09.05.18	A	Manchester City	1-3
13.05.18	A	Liverpool	0-4

18. Appendix B – Premier League Table 2017-18

	Team	Pl	W	D	L	F	A	GD	Pts
1	Manchester City	38	32	4	2	106	27	79	100
2	Manchester United	38	25	6	7	68	28	40	81
3	Tottenham Hotspur	38	23	8	7	74	36	38	77
4	Liverpool	38	21	12	5	84	38	46	75
5	Chelsea	38	21	7	10	62	38	24	70
6	Arsenal	38	19	6	13	74	51	23	63
7	Burnley	38	14	12	12	36	39	-3	54
8	Everton	38	13	10	15	44	58	-14	49
9	Leicester City	38	12	11	15	56	60	-4	47
10	Newcastle United	38	12	8	18	39	47	-8	44
11	Crystal Palace	38	11	11	16	45	55	-10	44
12	Bournemouth	38	11	11	16	45	61	-16	44
13	West Ham United	38	10	12	16	48	68	-20	42
14	Watford	38	11	8	19	44	64	-20	41
15	Brighton and Hove Albion	38	9	13	16	34	54	-20	40
16	Huddersfield Town	38	9	10	19	28	58	-30	37
17	Southampton	38	7	15	16	37	56	-19	36
18	Swansea City	38	8	9	21	28	56	-28	33
19	Stoke City	38	7	12	19	35	68	-33	33
20	West Bromwich Albion	38	6	13	19	31	56	-25	31